STRATEGIES for Content Area READING

LEVEL E

- **Primary Sources**
- **Science and Math Content**
- **Study Skills**
- **Content Vocabulary**
- **Test Preparation**

Options Publishing Inc.

Table of Contents

LESSON 1
Laura Ingalls Wilder and the American Frontier 5
Drawing Conclusions

LESSON 2
New Worlds Await 17
Identifying Main Ideas and Supporting Details

LESSON 3
Using Maps 29
Reading Maps

Math Connection

LESSON 4
A Clash of Cultures 41
Comparing and Contrasting

LESSON 5
Using Graphs and Charts 53
Interpreting Graphs, Charts, and Diagrams

Math Connection

LESSON 6
A Nation of Immigrants 65
Understanding Cause and Effect

Math Connection

LESSON 7
Energy: From the Wheel to the Stars **77**
Classifying

Math Connection

LESSON 8
Give Us Freedom **89**
Telling Fact from Opinion

LESSON 9
Understanding Documents **101**
Interpreting Political Cartoons, Photographs, and Documents

LESSON 10
Hernando Cortés **113**
Taking Notes

Assessment
Part 1: Multiple-Choice Test **125**
Part 2: Constructed-Response Test **131**
Part 3: Document-Based Question Test **135**

Glossary **141**

Product Development: Atlantic Group, Christine Lund Orciuch
Design and Production: The Quarasan Group, Inc.
Reviewer: John-Paul Bianchi, Social Studies Supervisor, New York City Board of Education
Editor: Carolyn Thresher
Production Supervisor: Sandy Batista
Cover Design: Alan Lee

Abbreviations are as follows: t=top, c=center, b=bottom, l=left, r=right

Photography Credits:
2 (t) ©Bettmann/Corbis; 2 (c) ©Corbis; 2 (b) ©New York Historical Society; 3 ©PhotoDisc, Inc.; 5 (border) ©MetaTools; 5 ©Bettmann/Corbis; 6 ©Corbis; 7 ©PhotoDisc, Inc.; 9 ©Bettmann/Corbis; 10 ©Library of Congress; 11 ©Buddy Mays/Corbis; 12 ©Bettmann/Corbis; 13 ©Courtesy of HarperCollins Children's Books; 14 ©Museum of the City of New York/Corbis; 15 ©Bettmann/Corbis; 17 (border) ©FPG International; 17 ©Corbis; 18 ©Corbis; 19 ©Corel Corporation; 19 (inset) ©FPG International; 20 (bear) ©Corbis; 20 (prairie dog) ©PhotoDisc, Inc.; 20 (big horn sheep) ©Corbis; 20 (bison) ©Corbis; 20 (snake) ©MetaTools; 20 (coyote) ©PhotoDisc, Inc.; 20 (bobcat) ©Corbis; 20 (map) ©Cartesia; 20 (elk) ©Corbis; 21 (squirrel) ©Corbis; 21 (deer) ©FPG International; 21 (fox) ©PhotoDisc, Inc.; 22 ©MetaTools; 23 ©Bill Ross/Corbis; 24 ©Corbis; 25 ©Andrew Brown/Corbis; 29 ©Cartesia; 30 ©PhotoDisc, Inc.; 34 ©Galen Rowell/Corbis; 36 (t) ©Lowell Georgia/Corbis; 36 (c) ©Corbis; 36 (b) ©Dave Bartruff/Corbis; 37 (t) ©Dean Conger/Corbis; 37 (c) ©Corel Corporation; 37 (b) ©Corbis; 41 (border) ©Corbis; 41 ©Bettmann/Corbis; 42 ©Bettmann/Corbis; 43 ©Corbis; 44 ©Museum of the City of New York/Corbis; 45 (t) ©Eliot Cohen & Judith Jango-Cohen; 45 (b) ©Corbis; 46 ©Bettmann/Corbis; 47 ©Buddy Mays/Corbis; 50 ©William S. Soule/Corbis; 51 ©Corbis; 52 ©MetaTools; 55 ©Corbis; 61 ©PhotoDisc, Inc.; 62 ©PhotoDisc, Inc.; 65 (border) ©Alexander Alland, Sr./Corbis; 65 ©Bettmann/Corbis; 66 ©Bettmann/Corbis; 67 ©Bettmann/Corbis; 68 ©Corbis; 69 ©Lewis Wickes Hines/Corbis; 70 (t) ©Hulton-Deutsch Collection/Corbis; 70 (b) ©Bettmann/Corbis; 72 ©Bettmann/Corbis; 74 ©New York Historical Society; 76 ©Corbis; 77 (border) ©Courtesy NASA; 77 ©Art Resource, Inc.; 78 ©PhotoDisc, Inc.; 79 ©Bettmann/Corbis; 80 ©Bettmann/Corbis; 83 ©Bettmann/Corbis; 84 (l) ©FPG International; 84 (r) ©MetaTools; 89 (border) ©Corbis; 89 ©T. Benincas/Amistad America, Inc.; 90 ©New London Historical Society; 91 ©Hulton Archive; 92 ©Bridgeman Art Library; 95 ©Slavery Library Archives, Talladega College, AL; 96 ©The Corcoran Gallery of Art/Corbis; 97 ©T. Benincas/Amistad America, Inc.; 98 ©Beinecke Rare Book and Manuscript Library, Yale University; 99 ©New London Historical Society; 100 ©Slavery Library Archives, Talladega College, AL; 101 (border) ©PhotoDisc, Inc.; 101 ©PhotoDisc, Inc.; 102 ©Corbis; 103 ©Library of Congress; 105 ©Library of Congress; 106 ©Bettman/Corbis; 107 ©Library of Congress; 109 ©A.J. Buck/Corbis; 110 ©Bettmann/Corbis; 112 ©Bettmann/Corbis; 113 (border) ©Getty Images; 113 ©Hulton Archive; 114 ©Bettmann/Corbis; 115 ©North Wind Picture Archives; 116 ©Charles & Josette Lenars/Corbis; 117 ©Bettmann/Corbis; 118 ©Historical Picture Archive/Corbis; 119 ©North Wind Picture Archives; 120 ©Art Resource, Inc.; 122 ©Bettmann/Corbis; 124 ©Michel Zabe/Art Resource, Inc.; 127 ©Cartesia; 131 ©Bettmann/Corbis; 133 ©Corbis; 136 ©Annie Griffiths Belt/Corbis; 138 ©Bettmann/Corbis.

Illustration Credits:
3, 60, 137 Ralph Canaday; 8, 31, 33, 35, 36–37, 38, 40, 79, 85, 93, 132 Gary Antonetti; 81 Cecile Duray-Bito.

ISBN 1-59137-032-9

Options Publishing Inc.
P.O. Box 1749
Merrimack, NH 03054-1749
TOLL FREE: 800-782-7300 FAX: 866-424-4056
www.optionspublishing.com

© 2003 Options Publishing Inc. All rights reserved. No part of this document may be reproduced or used in any form or by any means—graphic, electronic or mechanical, including photocopying, recording, taping and information storage and retrieval systems without written permission of the publisher.

All Rights Reserved. Printed in USA.

15 14 13 12 11 10 9 8

GETTING READY

Laura Ingalls Wilder and the American Frontier

LESSON 1

The Homestead Act of 1862 inspired thousands of people to travel West. They dreamed of owning a farm on free government land. The family of Laura Ingalls was one of these early pioneers. When Laura was sixty-five years old, she began to write stories about the joys and hardships of life on the frontier. Her books became the famous *Little House* children's series.

Think About Drawing Conclusions

Sometimes, an author wants you to draw a conclusion from what you read. When you **draw a conclusion**, you make a decision based only on the *facts* presented in the selection. Always look for the facts in the article that support your conclusion. "Laura Ingalls Wilder and the American Frontier" is an informational article. It gives you facts about Laura Ingalls Wilder, a famous children's author. The article also tells you about life on the American frontier. To draw conclusions about the information in this article, you should:

- Never make a guess. Make a conclusion, or decision, about what you read based only on the facts presented.
- Always look back at the selection to find the facts that support your conclusion.

Think About the Topic

Reread the short introduction above for "Laura Ingalls Wilder and the American Frontier." Write one fact from the introduction that supports this conclusion: *Settlers wanted to move West.*

_____
_____
_____
_____
_____
_____
_____

Drawing Conclusions 5

LESSON 1: Drawing Conclusions

STRATEGIES • TEST PREP
- Question
- Draw Conclusions
- Identify Sequence of Events
- Use Context Clues
- Compare and Contrast
- Use Study Skills

Question
To understand nonfiction, or informational articles, read all the headings. Then change each heading into a question. These questions help you understand what to look for as you read.

Laura Ingalls Wilder and the American Frontier

The Homestead Act

By the mid-1800s, both coasts of the United States were settled. Americans were now eager to settle the middle region of the country. In 1862, President Abraham Lincoln signed the Homestead Act. This law opened the Great Plains in the West to settlers. Any citizen who was the head of a family and over the age of 21 could get 160 acres of free land.

A typical homestead farm would be about the size of 145 football fields! In return for the land, settlers had to follow a few rules. They had to live on the land for six months out of every year. They had to build a home and raise crops. After five years, they would then own the land.

Thousands of families eagerly packed up their belongings into **Conestoga wagons** for the journey West. The Ingalls family was one of these pioneer families. They were the parents of Laura Ingalls.

✏️ WRITE HERE

Change the first heading to a question:
What was the Homestead Act?

Now answer the question.

© 2003 Options Publishing Inc.

6 Level E • Lesson 1

Life Was Hard on the Frontier

Settlers soon learned that life on the frontier was difficult. Many people came from towns and cities. They did not know much about farming. Their new land had never been plowed, so crops were difficult to grow. Settlers also faced other hardships. They suffered from **plagues**, terrible weather conditions, starvation, and sickness. Often, their farms did not make enough money to buy farm supplies.

In 1874, a plague of grasshoppers swept across Oregon, the Dakota Territory, Kansas, and Missouri. There were no poisons at the time to kill these insects. Grasshoppers piled three inches high in some places. They ate everything in sight. They ate the crops, the hair and skin of animals, clothing, and even each other! Many settlers were forced to leave their land. Some drew a picture of a grasshopper on the side of their wagons as a sign of why they were leaving.

During the winter of 1880–1881, blizzards came one after another. Winter lasted seven months. Snow drifted 40 feet high in some places and covered the railroad tracks. Trains carrying supplies to settlers could not get through. Many people and animals either starved or froze to death that year. There was no fuel for fires. All that was left to burn for warmth and cooking was prairie hay. People twisted the hay into large knots. They took turns feeding the knots of hay into the fire.

SOCIAL STUDIES

Conestoga wagon a large covered wagon with wide wheels. It was named for Conestoga Valley in Pennsylvania, where it was first made.

plague (playg) a very serious disease that spreads quickly to many people and often causes death.

Understand Conclusions

A **conclusion** is a decision you make based on the facts that you have read.

After reading this section of the article, what type of person do you think made a successful pioneer on the frontier? Use facts from the article to support your conclusion.

WRITE HERE

_____
_____
_____
_____

Drawing Conclusions

LESSON 1: Drawing Conclusions

The Ingalls Family Moves West

Charles Ingalls dreamed of moving West. He wanted land to start a farm. So, in 1869, he left the Big Woods in Wisconsin with his wife and two daughters, Laura and Mary. The family traveled by Conestoga wagon into Indian Territory. They settled near Independence, Kansas. Laura's father built a house and stable. But the family was forced to leave after they discovered their land still belonged to the Osage Indians. They returned to their old home in the Big Woods in 1871.

Laura's mother was glad to be home. But her father longed to go West again. In 1874, the Ingalls journeyed to Walnut Grove, Minnesota. They lived in a **dugout** on the banks of Plum Creek until Laura's father built a sturdy wooden house for them. They planted wheat, but a plague of grasshoppers destroyed their crop. Without any income from crops, they had to sell the farm.

dugout
a type of house made by digging out a cave from the bank of a creek. The back and sides of the house are the dirt walls of the cave. The front wall and door are made of logs, mud, and other materials.

Draw Conclusions Using a Map

Maps are a good source of information. They often show details that are not included in the text of an article. Maps organize information. Study the map and the different places in which Laura Ingalls Wilder traveled or lived.

The stars identify the places where Laura Ingalls Wilder lived during her life.

WRITE HERE

Use the map and what you know to answer the questions.

1. In what area, or region, of the United States did the Ingalls mostly live?

2. The Ingalls moved many times. What do you think life was like for Laura and her sister?

Several years of hardship followed for the family. But in 1879, they made their final move to the Dakota Territory. Laura's father was offered a job as a manager for the railroad. The Ingalls became the first residents of the new town of De Smet—the "little town on the prairie." Laura's mother insisted that they settle down in one place so that the children could go to school.

On February 19, 1880, Charles Ingalls filed his last homestead claim for 160 acres of land near De Smet. This town is in what is today South Dakota.

Laura finished school, and at the age of 15, became a teacher. In 1885, she married a local farmer named Almanzo Wilder. She and Almanzo settled in De Smet to raise their family.

Laura Ingalls when she was 17 years old.

SOCIAL STUDIES

Draw Conclusions Using Sequence

Sequence, or time order, is the order of events in a selection. Look for clue words, such as *before*, *after*, *then*, *finally*, *next*, and dates to help you determine the order of events. How do you think the Ingalls' lives changed after 1879?

WRITE HERE

Drawing Conclusions

LESSON 1: Drawing Conclusions

Use Primary Sources

A **primary source** is a record made by people who lived during an event. Old photographs, diaries and journals written at the time, and artwork are examples of primary sources.

This poster from 1870 advertises land for sale. In 1864, the government doubled land grants to the railroads. Railroad companies received 20 square miles of government land for every mile of track they laid. The railroads advertised their land for sale to the public.

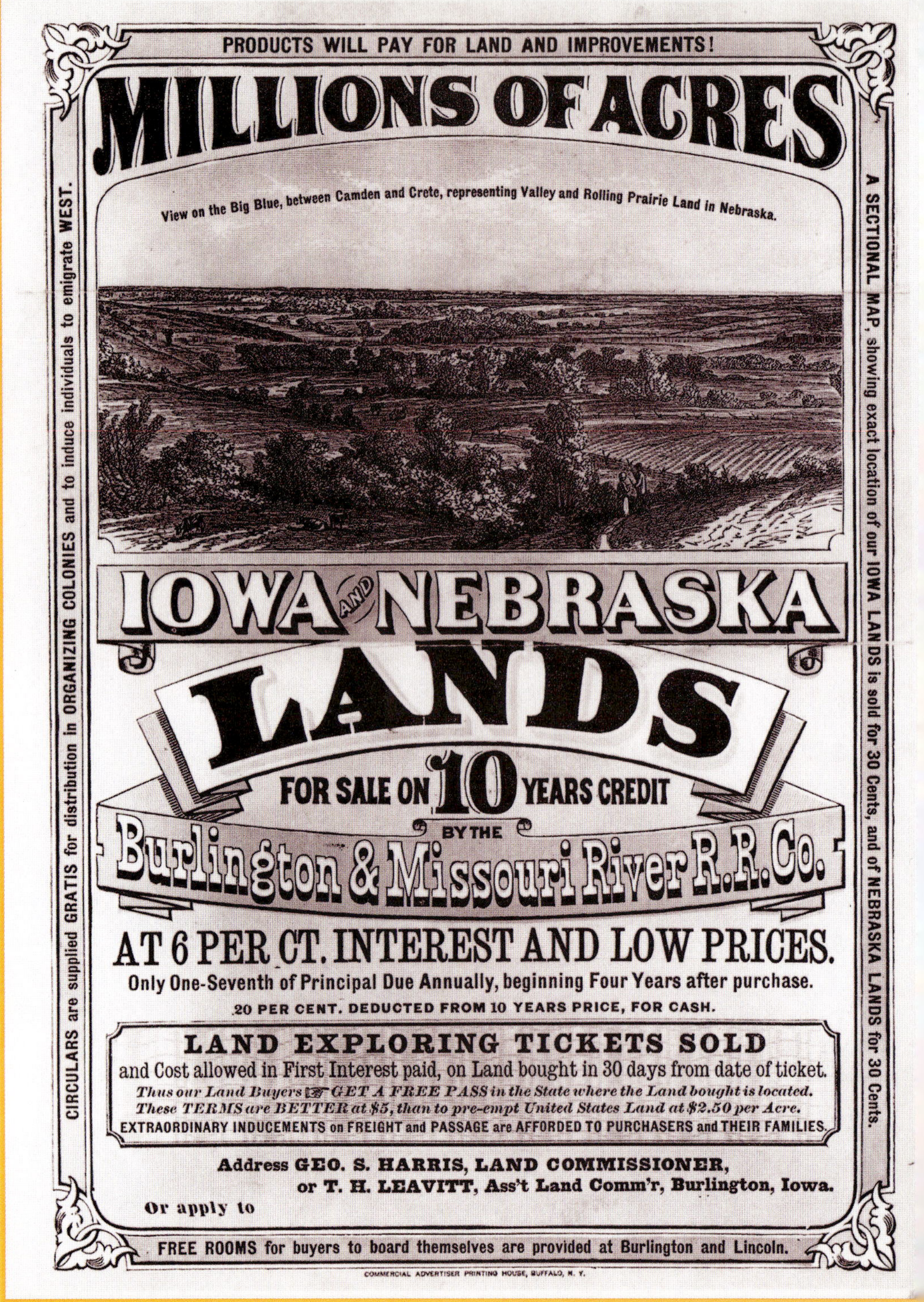

PRODUCTS WILL PAY FOR LAND AND IMPROVEMENTS!

MILLIONS OF ACRES

View on the Big Blue, between Camden and Crete, representing Valley and Rolling Prairie Land in Nebraska.

A SECTIONAL MAP, showing exact location of our IOWA LANDS is sold for 30 Cents, and of NEBRASKA LANDS for 30 Cents.

CIRCULARS are supplied GRATIS for distribution in ORGANIZING COLONIES and to induce individuals to emigrate WEST.

IOWA AND NEBRASKA LANDS

FOR SALE ON 10 YEARS CREDIT

BY THE

Burlington & Missouri River R.R. Co.

AT 6 PER CT. INTEREST AND LOW PRICES.

Only One-Seventh of Principal Due Annually, beginning Four Years after purchase.

.20 PER CENT. DEDUCTED FROM 10 YEARS PRICE, FOR CASH.

LAND EXPLORING TICKETS SOLD

and Cost allowed in First Interest paid, on Land bought in 30 days from date of ticket. Thus our Land Buyers ☞ GET A FREE PASS in the State where the Land bought is located. These TERMS are BETTER at $5, than to pre-empt United States Land at $2.50 per Acre. EXTRAORDINARY INDUCEMENTS on FREIGHT and PASSAGE are AFFORDED TO PURCHASERS and THEIR FAMILIES.

Address GEO. S. HARRIS, LAND COMMISSIONER, or T. H. LEAVITT, Ass't Land Comm'r, Burlington, Iowa.

Or apply to

FREE ROOMS for buyers to board themselves are provided at Burlington and Lincoln.

COMMERCIAL ADVERTISER PRINTING HOUSE, BUFFALO, N.Y.

WRITE HERE

Look at the poster and then answer the questions.

1. What conclusion can you draw about the land from the poster?

_____

_____

_____

2. Using facts from the article, compare how the railroad land grants were different from the Homestead Act.

_____

_____

_____

SOCIAL STUDIES

The Wilder Family

A year after they married, Laura and Almanzo had a daughter. They named her Rose. Farm life was difficult for the new family. Droughts and hailstorms ruined their crops. Almanzo became sick from working too hard. The family moved several times, but always returned to De Smet.

Finally, in 1894, the Wilders left De Smet, South Dakota, for good. For 45 days, they traveled 650 miles by covered wagon to reach the Ozark Mountains in Missouri. Laura kept a diary of this brutal, harsh trip. When they arrived, they found a small farm that had 40 acres of land. They bought the farm. The family lived in the small, windowless cabin that came with the land.

Laura named this farm Rocky Ridge. Over the years, Laura and Almanzo expanded the cabin into a large, rambling farmhouse. The couple grew corn and potatoes. They built a hen house and stable. With the money they earned from selling eggs, potatoes, wood, and wild berries, the Wilders bought a pig and a cow. Later, they bought more land. After a few years, Rocky Ridge had over 200 acres of land. The Wilders worked very hard at Rocky Ridge. They finally achieved their dream of owning a successful farm.

Trees surround the farmhouse at Rocky Ridge.

Use Context Clues

Sometimes, an author tells you the meaning of a new word by giving you clues in the words or sentences that surround the new word. One clue writers often give you is a **synonym clue**. A **synonym** is a word that means the same or nearly the same as another word. *Unhappy* and *sad* are synonyms.

WRITE HERE

Read this sentence from the article. Write the synonym clue the author uses to help you understand what the word *brutal* means. Then write another synonym for the word *brutal*.

Laura kept a diary of this brutal, harsh trip.

_____

Drawing Conclusions **11**

LESSON 1: Drawing Conclusions

manuscript
the original handwritten or typed pages of a book, poem, or piece of music before it is printed.

Draw Conclusions by Comparing and Contrasting

Comparing means to look at how people, places, or objects, are the same.

Contrasting means to look at the differences between people, places, or objects. Contrasting things helps you understand them better.

Life as a Writer

At Rocky Ridge, Laura was successful at raising chickens. She wrote many articles for magazines about farm tasks. The extra money she earned from writing helped pay for visits to her mother and sisters in De Smet.

Laura also told stories about her life on the frontier. Laura's daughter, Rose, enjoyed her mother's stories. Rose often asked her mother to write down these old family stories so they would not be lost.

In 1932, when Laura Ingalls Wilder was 65, she wrote a **manuscript** titled *Little House in the Big Woods*. She sent it to a publisher. When the book was finally published, it became a huge success. Children all over the world begged for more stories about Laura and her sister, Mary. The result was the *Little House* books. Before her death in 1957, Laura Ingalls Wilder achieved success as a farmer and as an author.

Ninety-year-old Laura Ingalls Wilder signs one of her children's books.

NET CONNECTION
http://www.lauraingallswilderhome.com

WRITE HERE

Use details from the article to explain the differences between Laura's life as a child on the frontier and her life at Rocky Ridge in Missouri with Almanzo.

Understand a Time Line

A **time line** is a diagram. It shows you events in the order in which they happened. Time lines help you understand and remember the sequence, or time order, of events.

Quickly look through, or skim, the article for dates. Add the events to complete the time line below. The time line is started for you.

1862   **1869**   **1874**   **1879**   **1894**   **1932**

1862 — President Lincoln signs the Homestead Act

1932 — Laura Ingalls Wilder writes *Little House in the Big Woods*

Drawing Conclusions 13

Drawing Conclusions

Draw Conclusions from What You See

Artists can draw pictures of real people, places, and things, or they can use their imagination. This 1867 Currier and Ives print called "The Pioneer's Home" shows the artists' idea of how a pioneer family lived. Study the picture carefully, and answer the question.

Do you think the print shows a true picture of pioneer life on the frontier? Use facts from the article to explain your conclusion.

SOCIAL STUDIES

Compare Yesterday and Today

Before Laura Ingalls Wilder wrote the *Little House* books, she wrote her memories of what it was like to grow up on the prairie. Use details from the article to compare and contrast life on the frontier with your life today. Organize your information by completing the Venn diagram below. The diagram is started for you.

Different **Same** **Different**

Frontier Life
- travel by wagon

- both have ways to travel

Life Today
- travel by airplane, car, train

Drawing Conclusions 15

Drawing Conclusions

🧩 Understand Drawing Conclusions

Imagine that you are a newspaper reporter in 1862. You want to inform people about the new Homestead Act. On the lines below, write a short news article that supports this conclusion: *The federal government wants to help citizens obtain free land.* Look back at the article for facts and information that support the conclusion.

The Washington Times

Washington, D.C.

written by _____

_____

_____

_____

_____

_____

_____

_____

_____

_____

_____

_____

Helpful Hint
Remember that good reporters answer the questions *who, what, when, where, why,* and *how* in their articles.

GETTING READY

New Worlds Await

Imagine what it must have been like to travel across America in the early 1800s. Travelers did not know what to expect. There were few books available to the public describing the different plants or animals. There was little information about weather conditions or the mountains, plains, or plateaus travelers would see. As people traveled from the Atlantic Coast to the Pacific Coast, what do you think they saw and experienced?

LESSON 2

Think About Main Idea and Supporting Details

The **main idea** is the most important idea in a paragraph. **Supporting details** give more information about the main idea. To find main idea and details:

- Look for the most important idea in a paragraph. That is the main idea. It is the most important idea you need to remember.
- Find facts and details in the paragraph that support the main idea. These details give the main idea meaning. They give you examples that describe the main idea.

Main Idea:
Travelers did not know what to expect.

↓

Supporting Detail:
Few books about plants or animals.

↓

Supporting Detail:
Little information about weather or land.

Think About the Topic

If you can predict what you are about to read, it is like having an outline in your mind. This helps you remember main ideas and details. Reread the short introduction above for "New Worlds Await." Next, look at the **headings**, **pictures**, and **maps** throughout the article on pages 17–28. What do you think the article is about?

_____
_____
_____
_____
_____
_____
_____
_____

Identifying Main Ideas/Details 17

LESSON 2 Identifying Main Ideas/Details

STRATEGIES • TEST PREP
- Question
- Identify Main Idea/Supporting Details
- Make an Inference
- Compare and Contrast
- Use Study Skills

Question

Asking yourself questions while you read helps you better understand what the main ideas are in the article. When you ask questions, you need to read carefully to find the details to answer your questions.

The author says that "Americans were on the move." I need to ask myself what facts in the paragraph support this idea.

New Worlds Await

"Westward Ho!" That was the new cry heard across the colonies in the early 1800s. **Americans were on the move.** They moved to the Spanish colony of Texas in the South. The Oregon Country in the Pacific Northwest drew hundreds of settlers. Many Americans believed it was the future of the United States to stretch from the Atlantic Ocean westward to the Pacific Ocean.

But travel in those days was not very easy. There were no buses, cars, or airplanes. And these early travelers faced something else very new to them. They passed through weather conditions they had never experienced before. They also traveled through **landforms** that were new to them.

Imagine you are an early settler. Many settlers came from England and settled in New England. This new world is not very different. England and New England are both areas that have temperate (TEM-pur-it) forests.

Temperate forests have a mix of trees. These areas have trees called deciduous (di-SIJ-oo-uhss). They lose their leaves in winter. Some of these trees are oaks, maples, and birches. There are also trees with needles that stay green all year round. These are called evergreen and **coniferous** trees.

WRITE HERE

List two facts in the first paragraph that support the main idea that Americans were on the move.

1. _____

_____

2. _____

_____

18 Level E • Lesson 2

deer

SCIENCE

coniferous (kuh-NIF-ur-uhss) an evergreen tree that produces cones.

landforms the different shapes that make up the earth's surface, including mountains, plains, canyons, hills, plateaus.

The temperature in a temperate forest is cool to cold in winter and warm in summer. The average rainfall is about 50 inches (127 cm) per year.

You might even recognize some of the same animals. Your new home in New England, like your old home in England, has foxes, squirrels, rabbits, birds, deer, and wolves.

Moving On

Now suppose that you and your family want to move to what is today called Sacramento in California. What weather and landforms do you think you might see?

As you travel, you will cross through five different biomes. A biome (BEYE-ohm) is a region of the world that is defined by its climate (weather) and the unique plants and animals that live there. To understand a biome, think of the plants, animals, and climate that are unique to where you live.

You and the other settlers gather supplies for the trip to Independence, Missouri. It is not easy. You'll go through temperate forests, pass over mountains, and travel over rough trails.

Understand Main Idea

In this part of the article, you will learn about biomes. An important part of a biome is its climate. **Climate** is the yearly pattern of average temperatures, rainfall, winds, and hours of sunlight in an area. The plants and animals are adapted to the climate there.

WRITE HERE

List three animals that you can find in a temperate forest biome.

1. _____
2. _____
3. _____

Identifying Main Ideas/Details

LESSON 2 Identifying Main Ideas/Details

North American Biomes

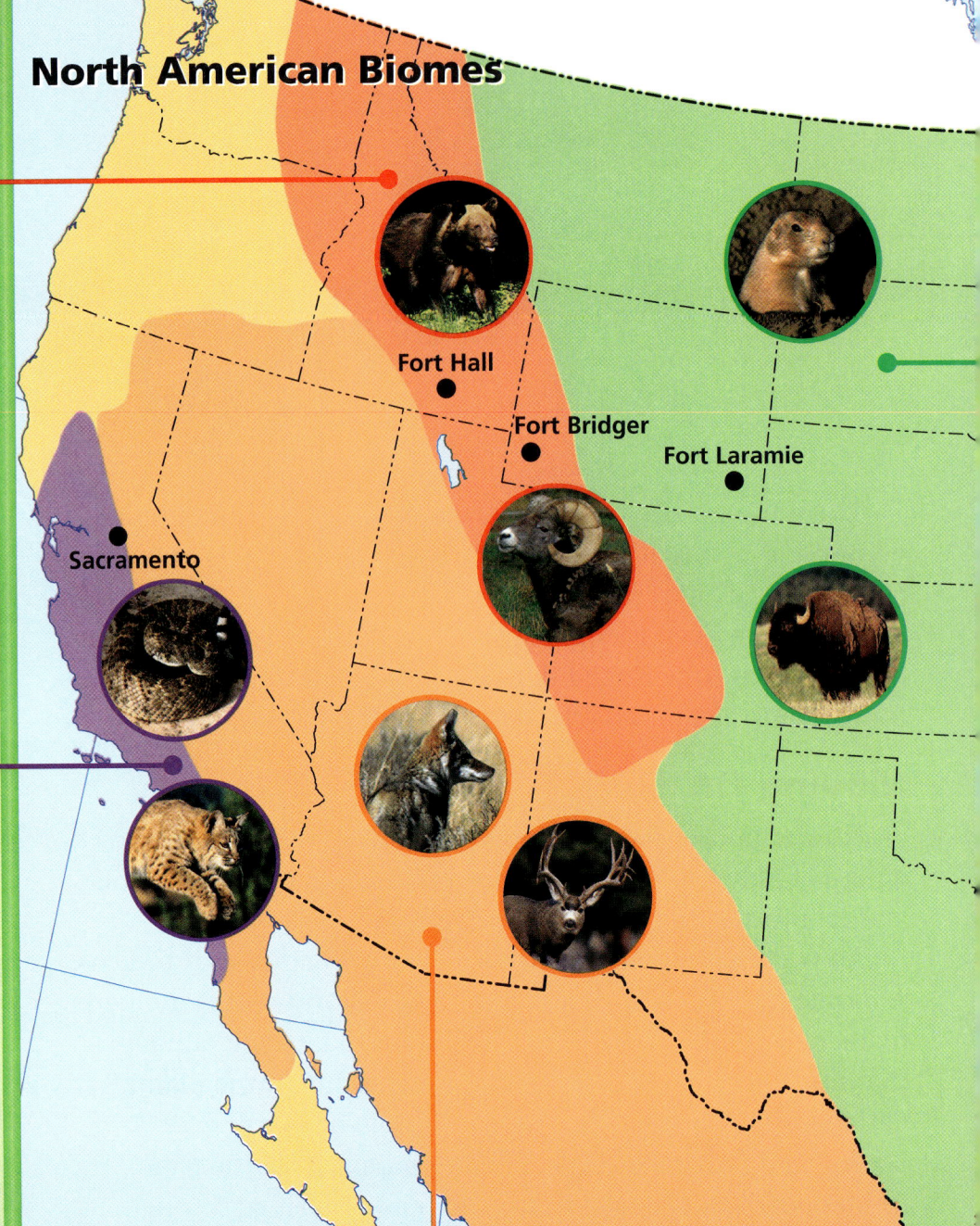

High Mountains
Many different climates, depending on location. Can have forests at the bottom and middle. The top of the mountain is cold with snow. Amounts of rain and snow vary.

California Chaparral
This area is also called the Mediterranean biome. Many shrubs, herbs, and grasses. Hot and dry in the summer. Winters are mild and rainy. About 12" of rain per year.

Desert
Extremes in temperatures with hot days and cold nights. Less than 10" of rain per year. Sagebrush, saltbush, and woody shrubs in the Great Basin. Southern deserts have cactus plants.

Key
- High Mountains ■
- California Chaparral ■
- Cool Grasslands ■
- Temperate Forest ■
- Desert ■

© 2003 Options Publishing Inc.

SCIENCE

Cool Grasslands
Prairies with tall, thick grasses. Cool in winter. Warm in summer. Drier than forest regions. About 30" of rain per year.

Temperate Forests
Mixed trees: trees that lose their leaves in winter and evergreens that stay green all year. Cool to cold in winter. Warm in summer. About 50" of rain per year.

• Independence

WRITE HERE

Study the map and answer the questions.

1. In which biome do you live?
   _____
   _____

2. Describe the climate in your biome.
   _____
   _____
   _____

Identifying Main Ideas/Details

LESSON 2 Identifying Main Ideas/Details

buffalo

Into the Grasslands

You have reached Independence, Missouri. Now you'll travel northwesterly to the Platte River, along the Oregon Trail. Your next stop will be Fort Laramie in present-day Wyoming.

The trip becomes more difficult. It will take five months by wagon to travel nearly 2,000 miles to reach California. You'll need many supplies. Travelers cannot buy flour, salt, corn meal, dried beans, sugar, or coffee on the way. Conditions will be difficult. You'll face heat, cold, wind, rain, dust, and mud. Perhaps the hardest part will be the thirst and hunger.

But this part of your trip will send you into a new biome, the cool grasslands. This region is drier than the temperate forests. It gets about 30 inches (76 cm) of rain per year. Now you see prairies with tall, thick grasses.

Farms, forests, and villages are gone. Tall, thick grasses surround you. When the wind blows, the grasses wave back and forth. Every spring beautiful wildflowers bloom for as far as the eye can see. The weather is cool in winter and warm in summer.

You'll also discover new animals. The plains have huge herds of buffalo, elk, antelopes, and deer. Look carefully and you'll see prairie dogs pop their heads up from their burrows beneath the ground.

You can't stay too long in the grasslands. <mark>You have to get through the mountain pass before winter. If not, you'll have to</mark>

Identify Main Idea and Details

Facts and **details** are important. They support and describe the **main idea**.

Look at the cluster map. The main idea is written in the middle circle. As you read "Into the Grasslands," fill in the blank circles with facts and details that support the main idea.

WRITE HERE

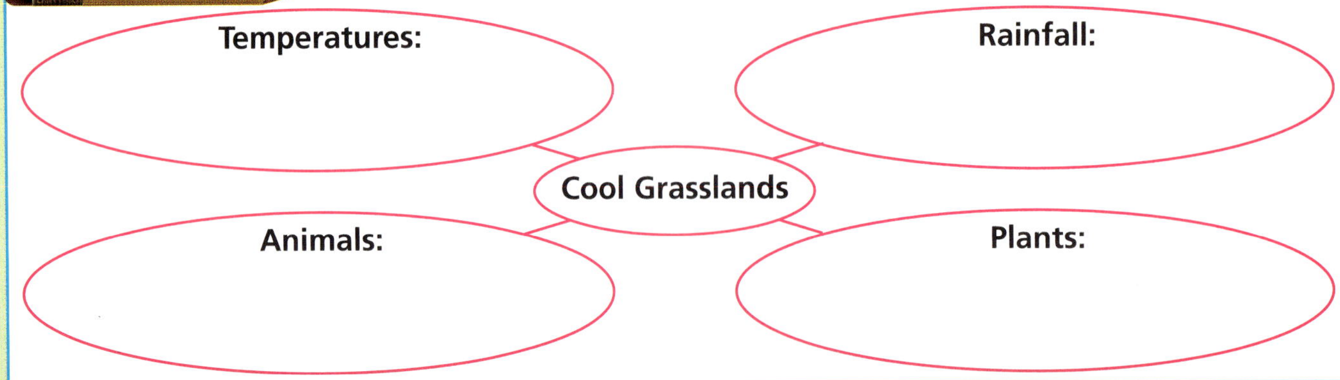

- Temperatures:
- Rainfall:
- Animals:
- Plants:

Cool Grasslands

stop traveling and wait until next spring. So, it is time to move on. Next stop is Fort Bridger and South Pass.

The Mountains and South Pass

Luckily, you and the other settlers can use South Pass. It is a wide valley through the Rocky Mountains in present-day Wyoming. Since South Pass is low, snow does not block it as often as it blocks higher passes. Because the pass is not as steep, wagons can travel through it.

As you look up, you see snow covering the tops of the mountains. The tops of the mountains are very cold. Very little grows there. Halfway up the mountains are cool, deep evergreen forests. Ponderosa pines, fir trees, and spruce grow here. Amounts of rainfall and snow vary.

If you look carefully, you'll spot some unusual animals. Look on the rocky ledges and you might see some bighorn sheep. Look near the forest and you might see one of the largest mammals, the grizzly bear.

Seeing a grizzly standing as tall as 8 feet and weighing about 1,500 pounds reminds you that it's time to travel on.

bighorn sheep

SCIENCE

Use Details to Make an Inference

When you **make an inference**, you use logical reasoning to explain events. Use supporting details and facts in the article to help you make that inference.

The author says that we must get through the mountain pass before winter. If not, we'll have to stop traveling and wait until next spring. I know that it is difficult to travel by wagon through the snow. I can infer that we cannot travel in our wagons through snowstorms: the wheels will get stuck in the snow.

WRITE HERE

Settlers traveling West used South Pass. List two *details* that tell you that South Pass is the best route through the Rocky Mountains.

1. _____

_____

2. _____

_____

Identifying Main Ideas/Details

LESSON 2: Identifying Main Ideas/Details

Use Details to Compare and Contrast

When you **compare** and **contrast**, you look at how things or ideas are alike and different.

Comparing and contrasting helps you understand the main idea in an article.

Notice that the author compares and contrasts the days and nights in the desert. The days are hot. The nights are cold.

Look back at the article for the facts needed to complete this chart. The chart is started for you.

The Desert

You made it through the mountains to Fort Hall (in present-day Idaho). You take a rest and get new supplies, especially water. You'll need it as you travel into the desert. Now it's time to pick up the California Trail.

As you approach the Great Basin, you see a huge desert. A desert biome usually gets 10 inches (25 cm) or less of rain per year. The days can be very hot. But the nights are very cold.

This area does not have the large cactus and yucca plants that you usually think of in a desert. The Great Basin is covered with sagebrush and saltbush. But sit quietly and you'll see a number of common desert animals. Look for mule deer, kangaroo rats, coyotes, red-tailed hawks, burrowing owls, lizards, and golden eagles.

Water for drinking and cooking is running low. It's time to move on to California.

coyote

WRITE HERE

Factors	Great Basin Desert Biome	Mountain Biome
Rainfall	10" or less	varies
Temperatures	hot days and cold nights	
Animals		
Plants		

Level E • Lesson 2

bobcat

The Mediterranean of the West

You've made it. You're in Sacramento. Just to the south of the city, you discover another biome. In the California chaparral (sha-puh-RAL), the winters are mild and rainy. The summers are very hot and dry.

The word *chaparral* comes from the Spanish word *chaparro*. It means "a thick growth of oak shrubs." Oak shrubs are plants that grow very close to the ground. The average rainfall is only about 12 inches (30 cm) per year.

The chaparral is only found in five places on the earth: coastal California, South Africa, Western Australia, Southern Europe, and South America. The California chaparral biome is the only one in North America.

By late summer, this area is so dry that it often catches fire. This process helps clear out old plants and improve the soil.

Look closely. You'll see bobcats, scrub jays, and even a mountain lion. After dark, you might see rattlesnakes. But don't take too long. You've reached the end of the trail. Now it's time to build a permanent home.

Think about the different biomes you've passed through. Dark, deep temperate forests, cool grasslands, high mountains, deserts, and the chaparral. Which was your favorite and why?

NET CONNECTION
http://www.enchantedlearning.com/biomes

Find Supporting Details

Supporting details are important because they give meaning to the main idea. They also help you remember the main idea by giving you examples.

The California chaparral (sha-puh-RAL) is a unique biome along the coast of California. The winters are mild and rainy. The summers are very hot and dry.

WRITE HERE

Skim the paragraph to find facts that support this main idea:
The California chaparral is unique, or special.

_____
_____
_____

Identifying Main Ideas/Details 25

LESSON 2
Identifying Main Ideas/Details

🧩 Understand a Diagram

In this article, you learned that climate helps define a biome. One element that defines a climate is the amount of rainfall that an area receives. Deserts receive very little rain compared with temperate forests.

A **diagram** is a drawing or a plan that explains or illustrates information. Diagrams help explain how things go together or how they work. The title tells what the diagram illustrates.

Study the diagram below about the water cycle. Then answer the questions.

The energy of the sun causes water in oceans, lakes, ponds, and rivers to turn into a gas called water vapor. This process of turning liquid water into water vapor, or gas, is called **evaporation**.

Water vapor rises and cools. It changes from a gas to a liquid in a process called **condensation**. This liquid is called **precipitation**, which falls back to Earth as rain or snow.

Water soaks into the ground. The groundwater is used by plant roots and animals that live in the soil. Some groundwater runs into lakes, rivers, and the oceans. Surface water also runs into bodies of water.

1. What does this diagram explain?

   _____

2. What process changes liquid water into a gas called water vapor? How does it work?

   _____

   _____

3. What happens after the water returns as rain or snow into the lakes, streams, and oceans? (Hint: Always follow the arrows in a diagram.)

   _____

SCIENCE

List Details About Your Biome

Use the chart below to list facts and details about the biome in which you live. Use the biome map on pages 20–21 to locate your area. Do a "biosurvey" by thinking about the plants and animals you see in your area. You may want to look up facts about your area in the library or on the Internet. Work in small groups with other students to discuss the types of trees, plants, and animals in your area.

Main Idea — My Biome

Supporting Details
- Temperature
- Rainfall
- Plants
- Animals

Identifying Main Ideas/Details 27

LESSON 2

Identifying Main Idea/Details

Describe Your Biome

Use the information from the chart you completed about the characteristics of the biome in which you live to write a description of your area. You may add drawings, pictures, margin notes, or examples of leaves found in the area. Be sure to include details and facts that add to your main idea: Your Biome.

Level E • Lesson 2

GETTING READY

Using Maps

LESSON 3

Maps help you find out about places. To read maps, you need to know what the symbols mean, to understand the shapes and colors, and to read all the titles. All these features form a picture that describes the location of a place.

Think About Maps

There are two basic types of maps: general purpose maps and special purpose maps.

General purpose maps show countries, cities, or continents as well as rivers, roads, and oceans. There are two types of general purpose maps: physical and political.

Physical maps show major natural features, such as mountains, rivers, and bodies of water, or the shapes that make up the earth's surface. **Political maps** show how people have divided up the earth's surface. These maps can show countries, divisions within countries, national borders, and the locations of cities and towns.

Special purpose maps can show climates, population density, or product distribution. To read a map, follow these steps:

- Look at the whole map and read the **title**. It tells you what the map is about.
- Look at the **legend**, or key. It tells you what the symbols on the map stand for.
- Look for the **compass rose**. This symbol shows you directions on the map.
- Look to see if there is a **map scale**. It is a line marked in miles, kilometers, or both. The scale shows distances on a map.

Think About the Topic

Use the information in **Think About Maps** to decide if the following maps are general purpose or special purpose.

Write either **General Purpose** or **Special Purpose** following each description.

1. A map of the mountains and rivers in the United States.

   _____

2. A map of where the greatest amounts of snowfall occur.

   _____

3. A United States map showing the borders of all the states.

   _____

4. A map showing where cotton is grown in the United States.

   _____

5. A map showing the population of the world.

   _____

Using Maps 29

LESSON 3: Using Maps

STRATEGIES•TEST PREP
- Question
- Read Maps
- Make an Inference
- Recognize Point of View
- Use Study Skills

Using Maps

General Purpose: Physical Map

A **physical map** shows major natural features. Look at the map of South America on the next page. You'll see that it shows elevations (how high mountains are and how low lowlands are), rivers, and water depth. The different shapes that make up the earth's surface are called **landforms**. A famous landform in South America is the Andes Mountains, a mountain range along the western coast.

Other landforms are plains and plateaus. A **plain** is a rolling, flat lowland. A **plateau** is also flat. But it is at a high elevation and rises steeply from the area that surrounds it. This map also shows elevations, or the height of the land from sea level. **Sea level** is the average level of the surface of the ocean, used as a starting point from which to measure the height or depth of any place. Look at the map on the next page. The differences in elevation are shown using different colors. The legend shows that land from sea level (0 feet) to 500 feet is dark green. Different maps use different color codes for elevations. Be sure to look carefully at the map legend.

Question

The first step for reading and understanding maps is to ask yourself questions. Read the title of the map on the next page. Ask yourself: *What is this map about?* The map shows you the natural features of South America. Study the legend at the bottom of the map. It tells you how high the mountains are and how low certain areas of land are. Study the map on page 31 and then answer the questions.

WRITE HERE

1. Look at the legend. If you wanted to go to the mountains in South America, would you go to the west coast or the east coast of South America?

2. Find Brazil on the map and look at its coastline. What is the depth of the water along the edge of Brazil?

30 Level E • Lesson 3

SOCIAL STUDIES

South American Physical Map

3. **Make an Inference:** How do you think life is different for people living in the Andes from those people living along the Amazon River?

4. Which region has the most farming? Use information from the map to explain your answer.

Using Maps 31

Lesson 3: Using Maps

General Purpose: Political Map

A **political map** shows how people have divided up the earth's surface. If you look at the map of South America, you can see that the continent is divided into several countries. Political maps can show countries, divisions within countries, national borders, and the locations of cities and towns. The map on the next page clearly shows the borders between countries and their capitals. The map does not show natural features.

Notice also that the map shows you latitude and longitude lines. These lines crisscross so that they look like a grid. It is used to help locate places on the earth. Of course, the grid does not really appear on the earth. People have made up the grid to show where places are located. This imaginary grid covers the entire earth. **Latitude lines** run east to west. **Longitude lines** run north to south. Both latitude and longitude lines are measured in degrees.

When measuring latitude, start at the equator, which is halfway between the North and South Poles. It circles around the globe and divides the earth into the Northern and Southern Hemispheres. The Equator is at 0°. Notice that the latitude lines above the equator are marked as **N** for north. Below the equator, they are marked **S** for south. Longitude lines divide the earth into the Western and Eastern Hemispheres. Look at the top and bottom of the map. Notice that the longitude lines are marked **W** for west. South America is in the Western Hemisphere.

WRITE HERE

Study the map on page 33 and answer these questions.

1. What is the longitude for the city of Manaus in Brazil?

   _____

2. How many countries are there in South America?

   _____

3. What is the capital of Brazil?

   _____

4. Name a major city in Argentina that is not the capital.

   _____

SOCIAL STUDIES

South American Political Map

Helpful Hint
When you look at a map, be sure to look for the legend, or key. That tells you what the symbols on the map mean. For example, a star shows the capital of each country.

WRITE HERE

5. What countries in South America does the equator run through?

6. What is the latitude for the city of Quito in Ecuador?

Using Maps 33

LESSON 3 — Using Maps

Special Purpose: Culture Map

Culture describes how groups of people act, how they live, what they eat, and what they believe. It also describes how people change their environment and create communities. Cultural regions are land areas where people share similar lifestyles. Notice that each region shows a similar climate. There are hot regions, dry regions, mild regions, and very cold regions.

Think about the climate in the region where you live. Is it hot, mild, dry, wet, or cold? The people in your region probably have some experiences that are similar to the ones you have. For example, if you live in a very hot region, your homes may look different from the homes of people who live in a very cold, wet region. The type of plants that grow in your area will also be different from the plants found in a very cold area. Think of the sports you play. In a tropical region near the ocean, you might go surfing. If you lived in a cold, snowy area, you might go sledding. Geography plays a large part in the lifestyles and similar experiences we share.

The culture map on the next page shows the major Native American culture regions, or nations, of eastern North America.

Make an Inference

Notice that the map on the next page divides eastern North America into regions, or nations. A nation is an area that has a common culture, ideas, and lifestyle. For example, there are Native Americans from the Eastern Woodland, the Plains, and the Southeast.

Inuit children wearing winter furs.

WRITE HERE

Think about the geography of the land. How do you think the culture of Native Americans living in the Eastern Woodland differed from the Native Americans living in Middle America? Use what you know and the map to support your answer.

_____
_____
_____
_____

© 2003 Options Publishing Inc.

SOCIAL STUDIES

Native American Cultural Regions of Eastern North America

WRITE HERE

Study the map and answer the questions.

1. List two neighbors of the Algonquin.

   _____

2. What is the name of the region where the Aztecs lived?

   _____

3. How many culture regions are named on the map?

   _____

4. What is the name of the people living in the Arctic region?

   _____

Using Maps 35

LESSON 3 Using Maps

Special Purpose: Climate Map

Another type of special purpose map is a **climate map**. **Climate** is the average weather in a place. This map shows the different climates of the world. The distance from the ocean, the latitude, and the elevation help determine a region's climate. Climate, or weather conditions, also affects where and how people live. This map shows six basic climates:

Polar climates
These areas are called tundra and ice cap regions. They get little snow or rain and are usually very cold all year.

Mild climates
These areas have rainy winters that are mild to cool. Summers can be warm to hot. These regions may be dry or wet.

Tropical climates
Areas that are tropical are hot all year. Some of these areas may be rainy all year, while others may have a dry season.

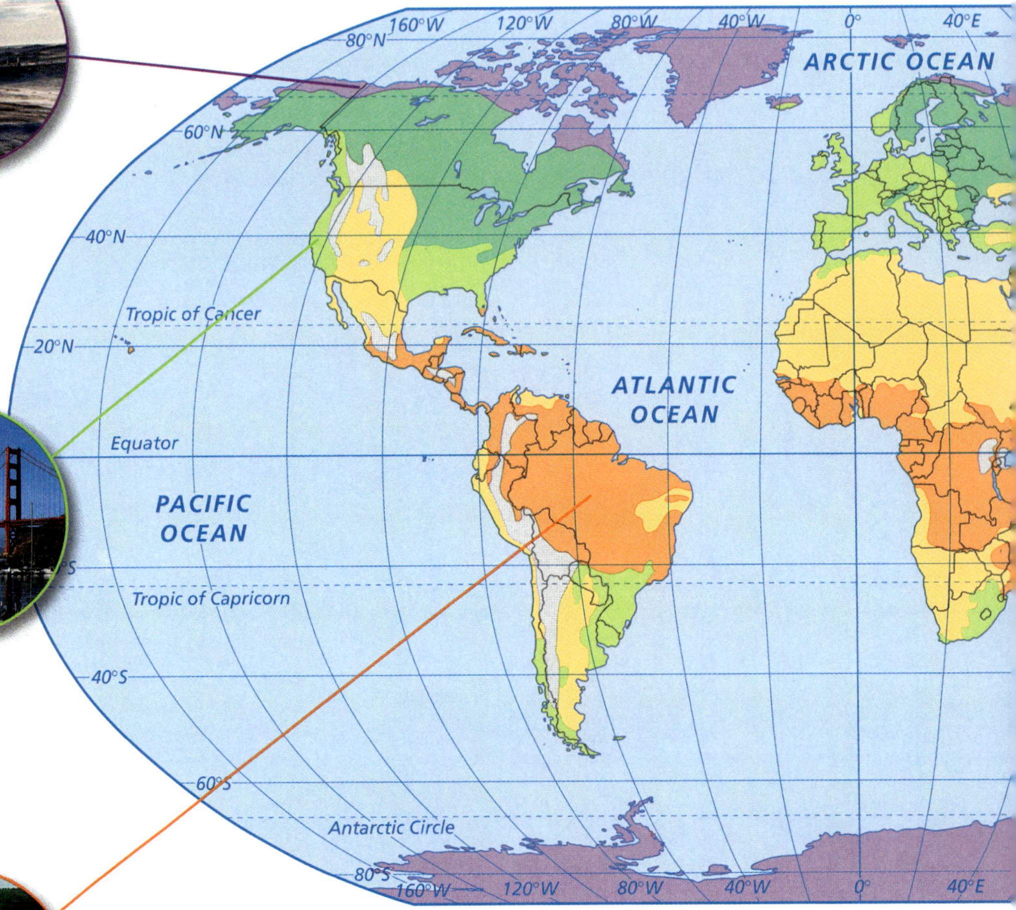

WRITE HERE

1. Look at the United States on the map. What climate type is shown for the area where you live?

2. Find the Antarctic Circle. Do you think the climate south of the Antarctic Circle is most likely to be wet and cold or dry and cold? Why?

36 Level E • Lesson 3

SCIENCE

Continental climates
These areas usually have wet summers that may be cool in some regions and hot in others. Winters are cold to very cold and snowy.

Highland climates
Elevation, or the height of the land from sea level, affects the climates of these areas. High elevations are colder than low elevations. Their distance from the equator also affects highland climates. Areas farther away from the equator are usually cold.

Dry climates
True deserts are very dry throughout the entire year. Some dry areas, such as semi-deserts are dry, but they may get occasional rain.

Climate Key
- Polar
- Mild
- Tropical
- Continental
- Highland
- Dry

Polar	Inuit village in Northwestern Territory, Canada
Mild	Golden Gate Bridge, San Francisco, California, United States
Tropical	Tropical Rainforest and Amazon River in Brazil
Continental	Trans-Siberian Railroad Tracks, Novosibirsk, Russia, USSR
Highland	Great Wall of China
Dry	Ayers Rock, Uluru National Park, Australia

3. Compare the photo of the Dry Climate area and the Polar Climate area. How does the climate affect the way the people live, what the people wear, and what the people eat?

Using Maps 37

LESSON 3: Using Maps

Special Purpose: Historical Map

Historical maps give information about a place as it was in the past. For example, if you had a historical Civil War map, it would show you where all the major battles were fought. Knowing how to read this type of map can help you gather and understand information. Historical maps add to the text you read and help show the information in a way that is easy to understand. Always look for the title and the date or time period for the map. Study the legend carefully to find out what the symbols or colors mean.

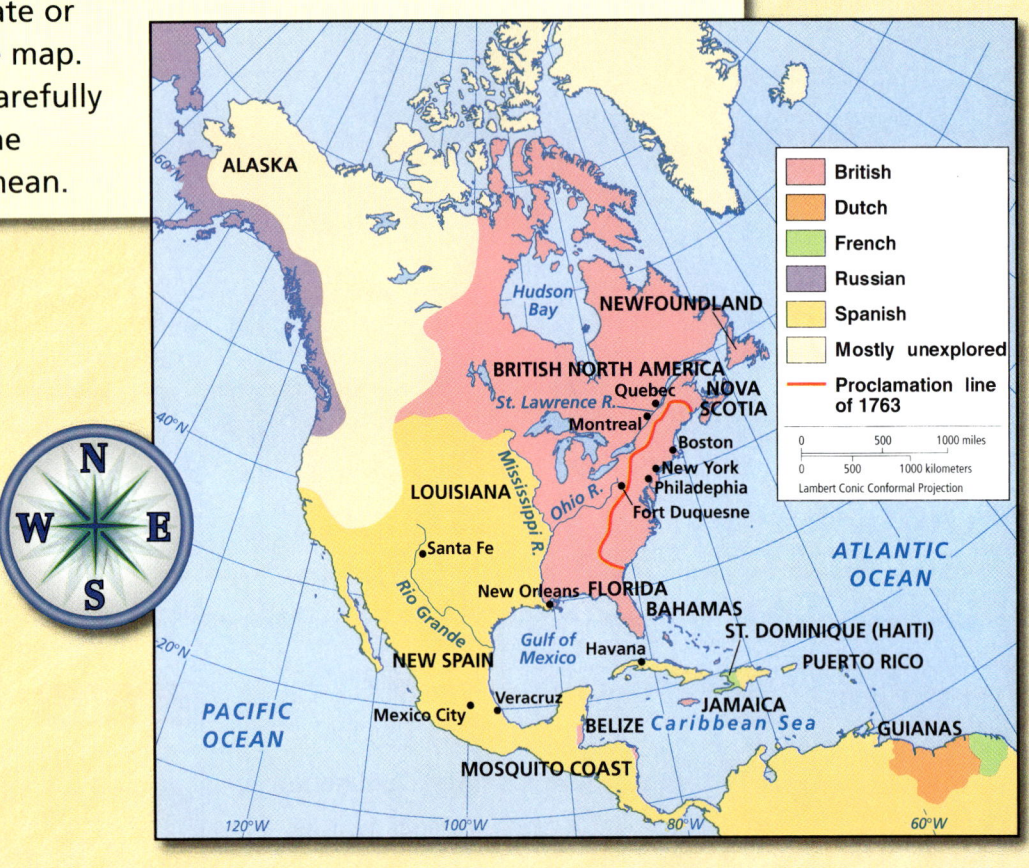

North America in 1763

WRITE HERE

Use the map and the article "The French and Indian War" to answer these questions.

1. What was the major boundary between British land and New Spain?

   _____

2. What country controlled the Great Lakes area?

   _____

3. How would the Proclamation of 1763 help Native Americans?

   _____

SOCIAL STUDIES

The French and Indian War

In the 1700s, France and Great Britain were the two most powerful nations in Europe. Both countries had important colonies in North America.

France owned Canada, all the land around the Great Lakes, and all the land west of the Appalachian Mountains. The French carried on a rich trade in furs in the Ohio River Valley. The British colonies also wanted to live and trade in the Ohio Valley. British colonists began to move into the area.

In 1756, Britain and France declared war. The French and Indian War had begun. The war is called the French and Indian War because most Native Americans in North America fought with the French against the British. The Native Americans felt the French trappers did not threaten their way of life. The British settlers, however, took their land.

In 1763, the British won. France had to give up almost all of its territory in North America. But some Native Americans continued to fight. They wanted to protect their land from British settlers. These uprisings worried the British, and they issued the Proclamation of 1763. This closed all the land west of the Appalachians to American settlers and hunters. The land was saved for Native Americans.

The colonists were angry. They did not believe in Britain's reasons for closing the land. The colonists thought that Britain wanted to control them by grouping the settlers together in the East. The split between Great Britain and the colonies began to widen.

Recognize Point of View

A **point of view** is an attitude, a viewpoint, or a way in which a person looks at or thinks about something.

Think about the British point of view and the colonists' point of view. Then answer the questions below.

WRITE HERE

This article describes the results of the French and Indian War. After reading the article, identify the point of view of each statement as either said by the British or by the colonists. Write either **British** or **Colonist** after each statement to tell whose point of view is expressed.

1. The colonists should have the right to settle on any land owned by Britain.

   _____

2. The colonists should not settle on lands west of the Appalachians.

   _____

Using Maps

LESSON 3: Using Maps

Special Purpose: City Map

Washington, D.C., has seen many changes over the years. It is the capital of the United States and home to the White House. In Washington, you'll find monuments and museums that explain our nation's history. Below is a city map of the area in Washington called the Mall. This type of mall is a large, shaded public walk. Here you'll find the Washington Monument and the Lincoln and Jefferson Memorials. If you visited the Mall, you may not know where to go to see the sights. A city map will help.

City maps show details of a small area. They usually show you interesting places to visit. Be sure to look at the **compass rose**. It tells you which direction is north, east, south, and west.

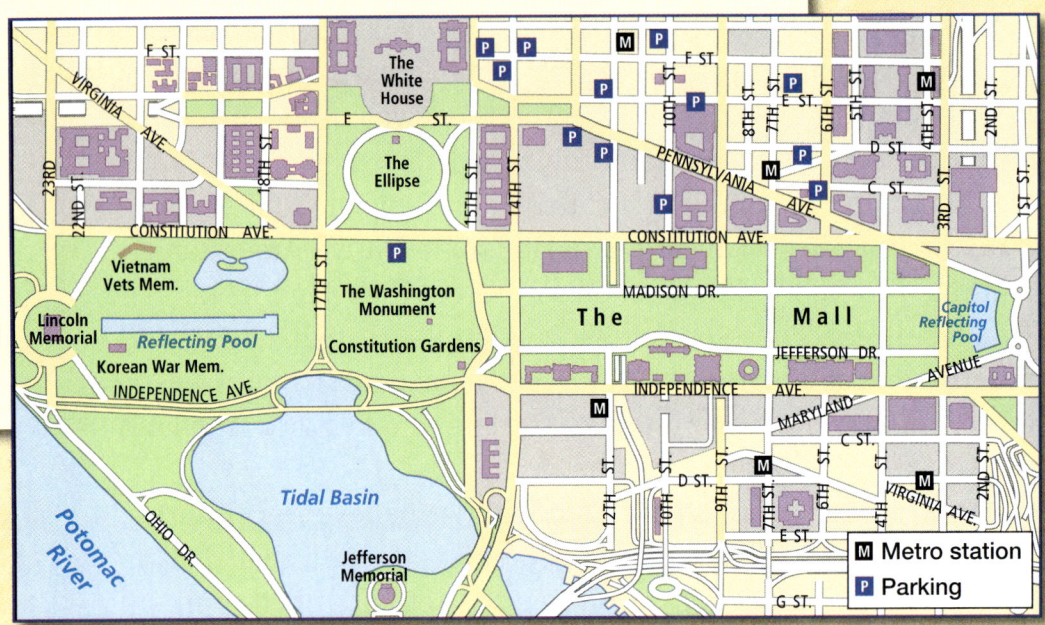

NET CONNECTION
http://www.lib.utexas.edu/maps/histus.html
and draw your own maps at
http://www.smartdraw.com

 WRITE HERE

Study the map and answer the questions.

1. If you were standing at the Jefferson Memorial, what is the fastest route to get to the Lincoln Memorial?

   _____

2. What is the closest Metro station to the Washington Monument?

   _____

3. If you were in Constitution Gardens, in which direction would you go to get to Constitution Avenue?

   _____

4. What is the symbol for "Parking"?

   _____

GETTING READY

A Clash of Cultures

European colonists arrived in America full of dreams for their future. Some colonists wanted religious freedom. Others wanted to become rich by trading or working the land. But Native Americans already lived here. Colonists and Native Americans had different ideas about the land.

Think About Comparing and Contrasting

When you **compare**, you find out how two or more things are alike. When you **contrast**, you look to see how they are different. By comparing and contrasting, you better understand what you read. For example, if you compare a football and a baseball, you might say they are both used in sports. If you contrast them, you might say they are different sizes, made of different materials, and used in different sports. To compare and contrast, follow these steps:

- As you read, look for topics that have something in common.
- Ask yourself: How are they alike? How are they different?
- Make a Venn diagram, two circles that overlap, to help you compare and contrast ideas or things. One part of the diagram lists details that are the same. Another part of the diagram lists details that are different.

Think About the Topic

When you **predict**, you make a statement about what you believe will happen. Predictions are more than guesses; they are based on what you already know about a person or an event.

Reread the short introduction above for "A Clash of Cultures." Make a prediction based on comparing and contrasting the colonists' views about the land with the Native Americans' views.

Colonists' Views:

_____

_____

Native Americans' Views:

_____

_____

Prediction:

_____

Comparing and Contrasting   41

LESSON 4 — Comparing and Contrasting

STRATEGIES • TEST PREP
- Question
- Compare and Contrast
- Make an Inference
- Recognize Point of View
- Draw Conclusions
- Use Study Skills

inhabitants
(in-HAB-uh-tants)
people who live in an area of land.

Question
Nonfiction writers help you learn new information by making connections or comparing and contrasting ideas with things you already know.

A Clash of Cultures

European Colonists Arrive in the New World

In 1620, an English ship called the *Mayflower* carrying 102 passengers landed in Plymouth harbor, which is located today in the state of Massachusetts. The passengers called themselves Pilgrims, and they had sailed from England in search of religious freedom.

The English colonists were not the first Europeans to arrive in North America. Since the late 1400s, the Spanish, Dutch, and French all came to the New World to explore and settle the land. They heard stories about a new land that was rich in animals and timber. European merchants found new opportunities for trade. Farmers found vast amounts of land for growing crops.

Colonists faced a problem when they arrived in America. By the time the colonists arrived, Native Americans had already lived on the land. Native Americans had been in the Americas for thousands of years before the first European explorers.

When Christopher Columbus landed in 1492, he called the **inhabitants** "Indians" because he believed that he had discovered the land of India. The early English colonists called them "savages," because Native Americans had a different culture, or lifestyle. They did not dress or look like Europeans or speak the same language.

WRITE HERE

Why did the colonists find the Native American culture so different from their own culture? When you compare and contrast ideas, look for answers in the paragraph and think about what you already know about the early colonists and Native Americans.

_____

_____

Ideas About the Land

Native Americans lived on the land and used its resources in many ways. Some Native Americans grew crops. Other tribes fished and collected shellfish for food. They hunted animals and gathered plants, seeds, and berries. Over thousands of years, Native Americans developed different traditions. Their customs, ideas, and beliefs are based on their use of the land.

Their ideas about the land and nature are closely related to their spiritual beliefs. They think of the land as a mother. The land provides people with life and food. Native Americans have a great respect for nature. Land, water, trees, and animals are for everyone to use. No one owns them. Native Americans believe they have a responsibility to protect the land.

To help understand these ideas about the land, think about the air. We cannot own or sell the air we breathe. Native American beliefs about the land are similar to these ideas about the air. Native Americans believed no one could own the land.

Europeans thought about land in a very different way from that of Native Americans. Europeans looked at land as something to be owned, tamed, and developed. They bought and sold land. Europeans judged others by how much land they owned. They dreamed of wealth by owning land and the resources on it.

Native American families enjoy the land surrounding their campsite along a river.

SOCIAL STUDIES

Compare and Contrast

When you **compare** and **contrast**, you look at how things or ideas are alike and different.

Comparing and contrasting helps you understand information in the article. Read the four paragraphs under "Ideas About the Land," and complete the lists below.

WRITE HERE

List 3 ways that Native Americans and colonists used the land in the same way.

1. _____
2. _____
3. _____

List 3 ways that Native Americans and colonists thought about land differently.

1. _____
2. _____
3. _____

Comparing and Contrasting

LESSON 4: Comparing and Contrasting

The First Hard Winter

The first winter of 1621 in Plymouth was very hard for the Pilgrims. They were afraid that the Native Americans would attack them. The weather was very cold. Their primitive houses did not protect them well. There was barely any food and not much fresh water. Many people became sick and almost half of the colony died.

Two Native Americans, Squanto (SHWAN-toh) and Samoset (sam-OH-set), rescued the starving colonists. Seven years before the Pilgrims landed, English fishermen had captured Squanto. The captain brought him to Europe and sold him as a slave. Later, Squanto gained his freedom. He sailed to Newfoundland, in Canada, on board an English ship. From there, he found his way home.

Samoset lived in what is now called Maine, the northernmost state in the Northeast. He learned a few English words from English fishermen in Maine. Samoset was on a hunting trip when he discovered the Pilgrims in Plymouth (Massachusetts).

Pilgrims give thanks for their safe landing in Plymouth, Massachusetts, on December 22, 1620.

Compare and Contrast to Make an Inference

When you **make an inference**, you make a logical guess based on the information you are given. You use information and details from the article along with your common sense and knowledge.

WRITE HERE

How might the Pilgrims have felt as they compared their old lives to their new lives in America? Why?

_____
_____
_____
_____

Contrast Primary Sources

A **primary source** is a record made by people who lived during an event. Old photographs, diaries and journals written at the time, and artwork are examples of primary sources. The selection below is from a primary source. It is part of a journal called "Mourt's Relation." It was written by people who arrived on the *Mayflower*. While exploring the area, these colonists found a Native American dwelling. Here is their description:

A Native American home and the interior of a colonist's home.

November 1620. The houses were made with long young sapling trees, bended [bent] and both ends stuck into the ground. They were made round like an arbor [arch] and covered down to the ground with thick . . . mats [made of straw and reeds]. The door was not over a yard high. . . . The chimney was a wide-open hole in the top, which they had a mat to cover when they pleased. One might stand and go upright in them. In the midst of them were four little stakes knocked into the ground and small sticks laid over, on which they hung their pots and what they had to seethe [cook]. Round about the fire they lay on mats, which are their beds. The houses were double-matted, for as they were matted without [these straw and reed mats covered the inside and outside walls]. In the houses we found wooden bowls, trays and dishes, earthen pots, hand-baskets of crab shells wrought (joined) together.

Using the pictures and the journal entry, contrast the Native American houses with colonial houses. How are they different?

_____

_____

_____

_____

Comparing and Contrasting

LESSON 4: Comparing and Contrasting

Make an Inference

An **inference** is based on the details and information in the article and what you know about an event or about human nature. After reading this section of the article, "The First Hard Winter," why do you think Squanto and Samoset helped the Pilgrims?

Squanto and Samoset spoke English. With their help, the Pilgrims could speak with other natives. The natives and colonists became friends. In 1621, the Pilgrims signed a peace treaty with Massasoit (mass-uh-SOY-et), chief of the Wampanoag (wam-PAH-oh-agh). Massasoit gave the Pilgrims permission to live on the 12,000 acres of land that became the Plymouth Plantation. But he did not understand the European idea of owning land. He believed in the native idea of sharing.

Squanto stayed with the Pilgrims for a year. He and other natives taught the colonists how to fish, raise corn, beans and other crops, and trap wild game. The Pilgrims were grateful for their help. In the fall, the colonists invited the natives to share in their first harvest. Massasoit and ninety of his men brought five deer. They celebrated their friendship with a three-day festival to show thankfulness for their survival.

Native Americans and colonists celebrate a thanksgiving feast together. This is how the artist imagined the event.

WRITE HERE

List two details that support your inference.

1. _____

_____

2. _____

_____

46 Level E • Lesson 4

Ideas About Wealth

The way the natives treated the Pilgrims is an example of their beliefs. They shared their skills, their food, and their land with the colonists. But as more and more settlers came from Europe, problems developed. Colonial settlements in the Northeast grew larger. They grew into villages and then into towns and finally into cities. The settlers wanted more land to farm and to develop. Colonists added to their wealth by gaining more land.

Native Americans used different types of shells for wampum.

Many East Coast tribes traded with the English colonists. Native Americans often used **wampum** or goods as money. They also traded furs, such as beaver, for goods from the settlers. When colonists wanted to buy land from the natives living there, they often traded goods.

In 1624, Dutch colonist Peter Minuit arrived on Manhattan Island. Today, New York City is located on Manhattan Island. Minuit wanted to buy land from the Man-a-hat-ta Indians. He gave them two cases of goods. These goods were probably some metal pots, cloth, hatchets, and beads. They were worth about $24.00. In return for the goods, the natives gave him the use of Manhattan Island.

Peter Minuit "bought" the island of Manhattan from the natives. But they did not understand the idea of "buying" or "selling" land. To the Native Americans, buying the land was like buying the air. They didn't realize that the Dutch now owned the land. The Dutch now had the right to force the natives to leave their homes.

SOCIAL STUDIES

wampum
(WAHM-puhm) beads made from polished shells, often used as money.

Compare and Contrast Points of View

Point of view is an attitude or a way in which a person looks at or thinks about something.

Read "Ideas About Wealth." Compare and contrast the colonists' point of view about wealth with the Native Americans' point of view.

WRITE HERE

Colonists' Views About Wealth:

_____
_____
_____

Native Americans' Views About Wealth:

_____
_____
_____

Comparing and Contrasting

Lesson 4: Comparing and Contrasting

Colonists Move West

As America grew, the colonists needed more land. They began to explore and claim more and more territory. Tension increased between the colonists and Great Britain. Finally, in 1776 the colonists declared war with Britain. America wanted independence from British rule.

The American Revolution lasted until 1783. The end of the war brought independence to the American colonies. When the peace agreement was signed in 1783, all the British lands south of Canada became a part of America. In the minds of Americans, this included the land where Native Americans lived.

Westward expansion continued. Settlers wanted more land to farm and raise cattle. There was less land for Native Americans. Conflicts between the two groups grew.

To end the fighting, Native Americans were forced to sign treaties with the Americans. The Congress of the United States signed peace treaties with individual tribes. These agreements divided the land between the tribe and the American government. But land became more and more valuable. Native Americans were forced to give up their rights to the land. They were forced to move to reservations, land that was set aside by the government for Native Americans. The land where they and their ancestors had once freely farmed, fished, and hunted was no longer their own.

Draw Conclusions

When you **draw a conclusion**, you make a judgment based on the facts presented in the article. A conclusion is always based on facts. The facts in the article support the conclusion.

NET CONNECTION
http://www.si.edu/nmai (National Museum of the American Indian)
http://www.plimoth.org

WRITE HERE

Using facts from the selection, why did the American government believe it was necessary to move Native Americans to reservations?

_____
_____
_____

SOCIAL STUDIES

Compare and Contrast Using a Venn Diagram

A **Venn diagram** is a good tool for comparing and contrasting information. The ways in which two things are alike are written in the middle, where the two circles overlap. Things that are common just to Native Americans are written on the left. Things common just to Early Colonists are written on the right. Complete the Venn diagram by listing facts from the list below. Look back at the article if you are unsure about where to list a fact. The diagram is started for you.

Facts About Native Americans and Early Colonists

- wanted opportunities for trade
- farmed land and grew crops
- hunted birds and animals
- built wealth by owning land
- believed they should protect the land
- respected nature
- bought and sold land

Different   **Alike**   **Different**

Native Americans
- believed they should protect the land

Alike
- farmed land and grew crops

Early Colonists
- wanted opportunities for trade

Comparing and Contrasting   **49**

LESSON 4: Comparing and Contrasting

Compare and Contrast Primary Sources

As you learned, a **primary source** is a record made by people who lived during an event. In 1870, William Soule photographed this Native American camp. It shows the Arapaho (uh-RAH-puh-hoh), living in the plains region, sitting around their campsite. Their dwellings are in the background. Buffalo meat for food and hides for clothing and shelter are drying on lines in the sun.

Arapaho Camp with Buffalo Meat, Near Fort Dodge, Kansas

Based on the introduction and photo above, what evidence is there that buffalo were important to Native Americans? Include as many details as you can.

_____

_____

_____

_____

SOCIAL STUDIES

Compare and Contrast Primary Sources

As the railroads moved west, huge herds of buffalo roamed the land. The herds were often divided by the railroad tracks, which the buffalo had to cross. The railroads invited hunters to kill buffalo for sport and money.

Killing Buffalo for Pleasure

1. Study the picture. Why were the men killing the buffalo?

2. This picture and the photograph on page 50 show a point of view, or attitude, toward buffalo. Compare and contrast the two pictures. How did the settlers' purpose for killing the buffalo differ from the Native Americans' purpose?

Comparing and Contrasting

LESSON 4: Comparing and Contrasting

Compare and Contrast by Writing a Journal

A journal describes activities and events as they happen. It might include facts about the weather, events that happened, or interesting people. Imagine that the year is 1621, and you were one of the passengers on the *Mayflower*. You have lived in the colony for a year. Write a journal entry that describes how your European values are different from the Native Americans' values. You may want to focus on clothing, food, shelter, and ideas about the land.

November 1621

_____
_____
_____
_____
_____
_____
_____
_____
_____
_____
_____
_____
_____
_____

GETTING READY

Using Graphs and Charts

LESSON 5

Graphs and charts organize information into a form that is easy to read and to understand. It is important to know what the symbols mean, to understand the shapes and colors, and to read the titles. These skills help you understand information in graphs and charts.

Think About Graphs and Charts

Graphs and **charts** are tools used to organize information about history and economics. They show information, or data, in a picture. Imagine that you wanted to know which five states recycle the most glass, plastic bottles, metal cans, paper, and cardboard. New Jersey recycles 56% of its recyclable materials. Wisconsin is next at 50%. Minnesota recycles 41%. Florida recycles 40%. Maine is the fifth state and recycles 35%. It is hard to remember all these percentages and organize them in your mind. Now look at the same data in a bar graph.

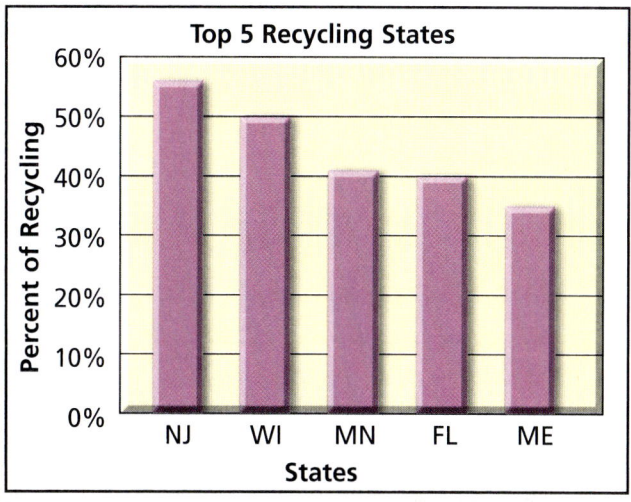

You can quickly see which state recycles the most by looking at the height of the bars. To read a graph, follow these steps:

- Look at the whole graph and read the **title**. This tells you what the graph is about.
- If the graph has a **legend**, or key, study it. It tells you what the symbols or colors stand for.
- Always read the **labels** in the graph. These tell you how the information is organized.

Think About the Topic

Use the information in **Think About Graphs and Charts** to answer this question:

What other types of information would best be shown in a graph or a chart? List two examples.

1. _____

2. _____

Using Graphs and Charts 53

LESSON 5
Using Graphs and Charts

STRATEGIES • TEST PREP
- Read Diagrams
- Read Graphs and Charts
- Use Study Skills

Understand Diagrams

A **diagram** is a drawing or a plan that explains or illustrates information. Diagrams help explain how things go together or how they work. The title tells what the diagram illustrates. Some diagrams also include a legend that shows what the symbols in the drawing mean.

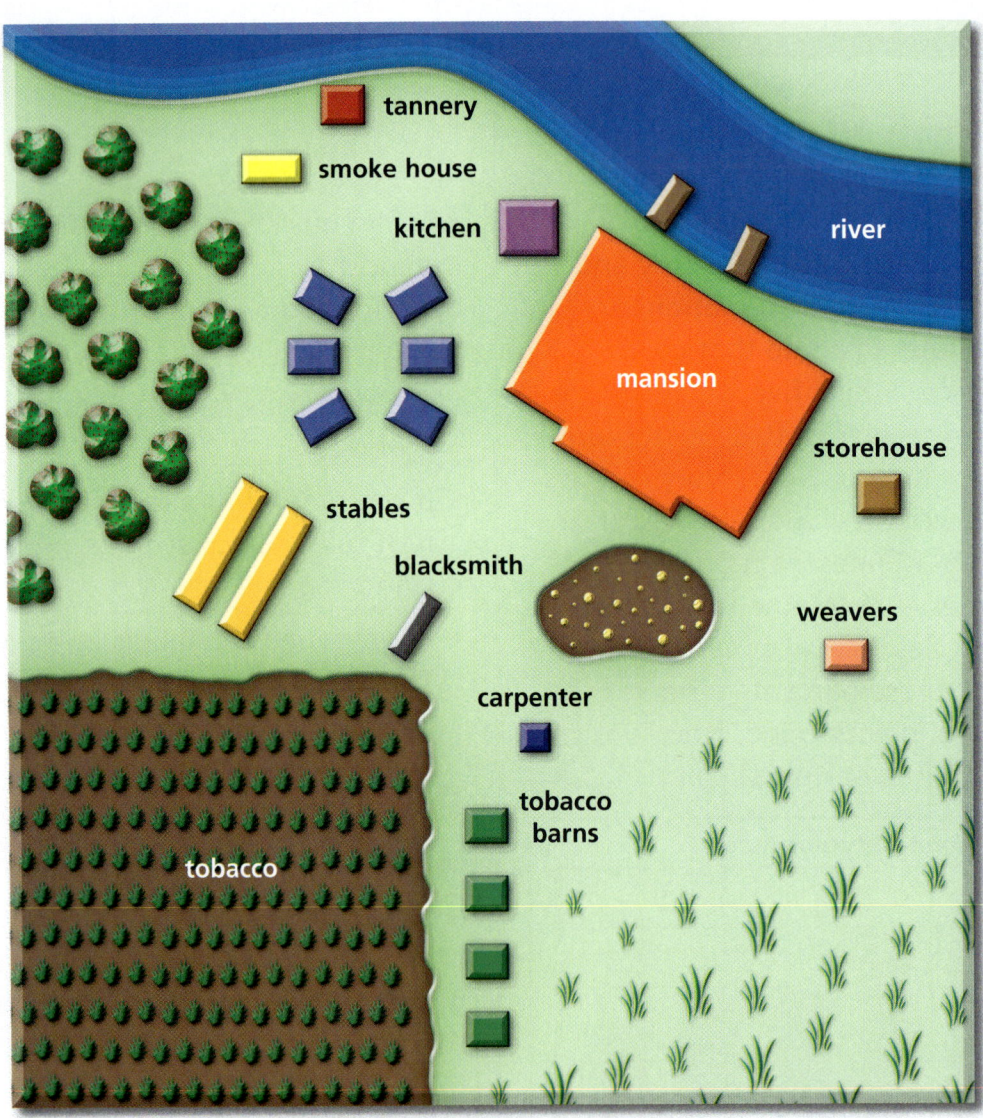

Plan of a Typical Southern Plantation

Legend: Cherry Orchard, Slave Buildings, Pasture, Docks, Gardens

54 Level E • Lesson 5

SOCIAL STUDIES

WRITE HERE

Study the diagram and answer the questions.

1. Carefully study the diagram. Circle the letter of the statement that is the best conclusion about a Southern plantation.

   a. The plantation was self-sufficient, or able to take care of the people's needs without much help from others.

   b. The plantation needed goods and products, such as clothing and food, from people outside the plantation.

2. What was a typical Southern plantation's largest crop?

   _____

3. Why do you think the kitchen was a separate building and not inside the house?

   _____
   _____
   _____

4. Look at the legend. Describe the symbol used to represent pastures.

   _____
   _____

Using Graphs and Charts 55

LESSON 5: Using Graphs and Charts

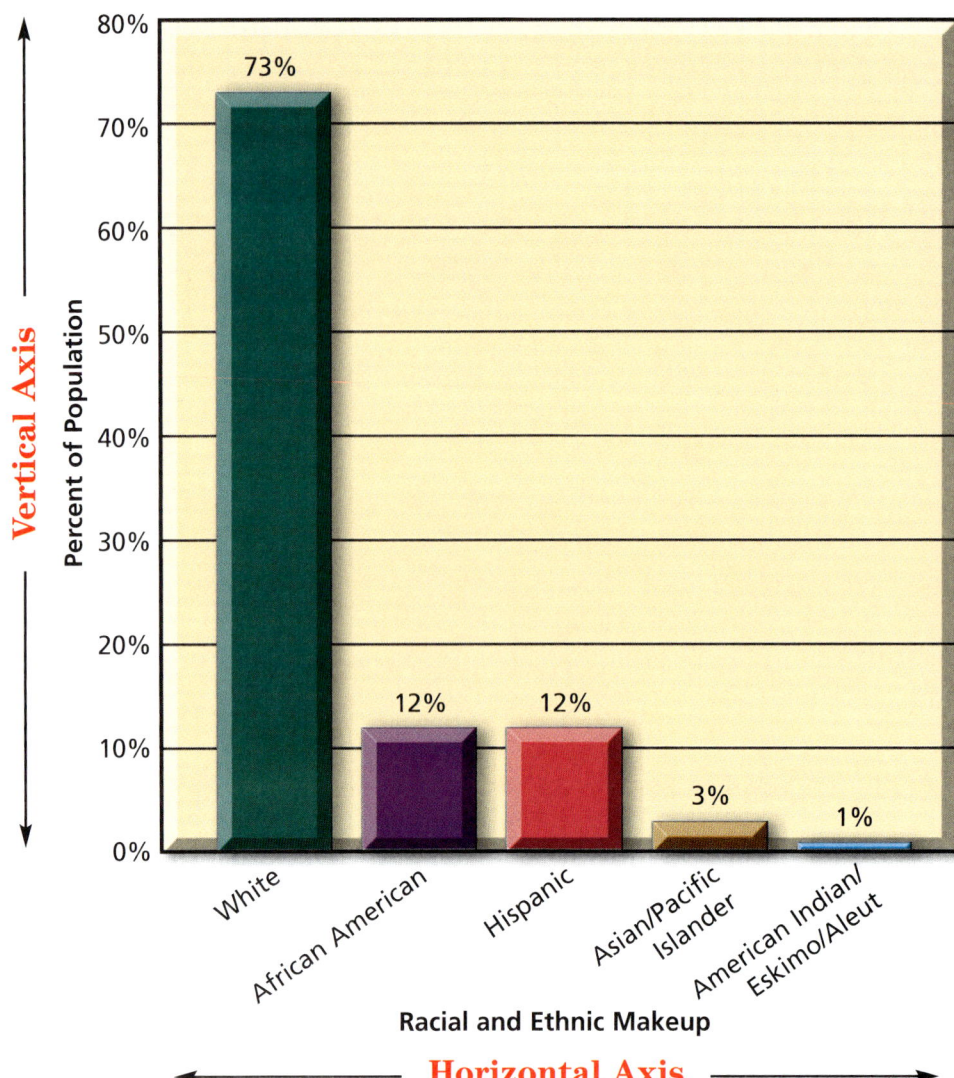

Understand Bar Graphs

A **bar graph** uses columns to show information. It has two labels. One label is next to a scale of numbers that tell you how much or how many. See the **vertical axis** on the graph. The other label along the bottom tells you the subject of the graph. See the **horizontal axis** on the graph.

Bar graphs can be vertical (top to bottom) like the one at the right. Or they can be horizontal (left to right).

WRITE HERE

Study the bar graph and answer these questions.

1. It is important to read the labels on a graph so that you understand what the numbers and percentages mean.

   What does the vertical axis tell you?

   _____

   What does the horizontal axis tell you?

   _____

2. Is more of the population of the United States made up of Asian/Pacific Islanders or African Americans?

   _____

3. Based on the graph, circle the letter of the statement below that is true about the makeup of the population of the United States.

   a. American Indian/Eskimo/Aleut make up more of the population of the United States than Hispanics.

   b. Whites make up more of the population of the United States than Asian/Pacific Islanders.

56 Level E • Lesson 5

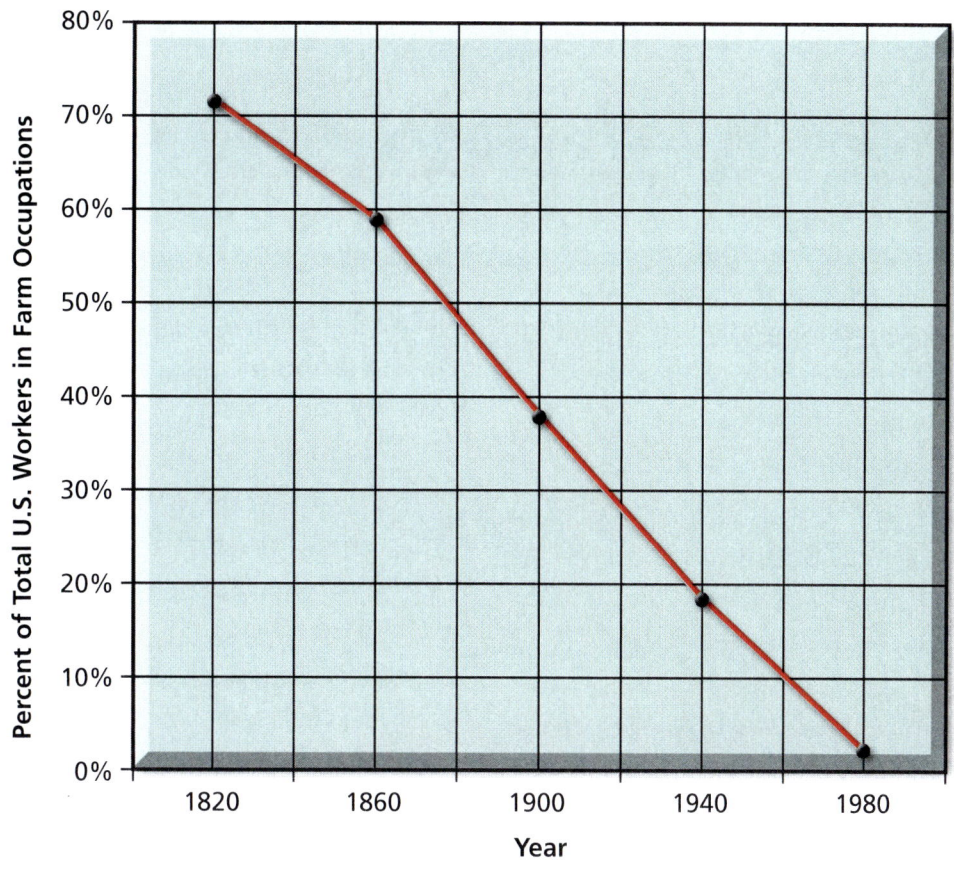

SOCIAL STUDIES

Understand Line Graphs

Line graphs, like bar graphs, show the relationship between two things. These graphs are often used to show trends, or how things are changing. To understand line graphs, always read the **title**. It identifies the main idea of the graph. Read the labels for the vertical axis and the horizontal axis. In this graph, the vertical axis tells you the percentage of workers in farm occupations. The horizontal axis along the bottom tells you the years covered in the graph. Notice that the data was collected every forty years. For example, there are forty years between 1820 and 1860.

Source: U.S. Department of Agriculture, Economic Research Service

WRITE HERE

1. What time period does the graph cover?

2. In 1900, about what percent of the population worked in farm-related jobs?

3. Look at the graph. Think about what it shows you about farm workers. Use facts from the graph to draw a conclusion. Can you conclude that there are more farms or fewer farms in 2000? Why?

Using Graphs and Charts **57**

LESSON 5: Using Graphs and Charts

Understand Tables

Tables, or charts, list information, usually in columns. Tables organize many facts into a small amount of space. You can find tables and charts in your social studies, math, and science textbooks. One example of a table is in the front of this book: the Table of Contents. This table identifies the parts of the book. Tables of Contents also help you find page numbers quickly.

Look at the table below. It shows you how the population of cities grew over time.

How the Cities Grew

Before 1870, most people lived on farms. But as the United States grew and opened more factories in the cities, many people moved from the farms to the cities. Immigrants to the United States also moved to cities to find work in these factories.

This table shows you the population growth of cities. To quickly see that growth, turn the table into a bar graph. The first column, or bar, is done for you.

How the Cities Grew	
Year	% of U.S. Population Living in Cities
1880	28%
1910	45%
1940	56%
1970	75%

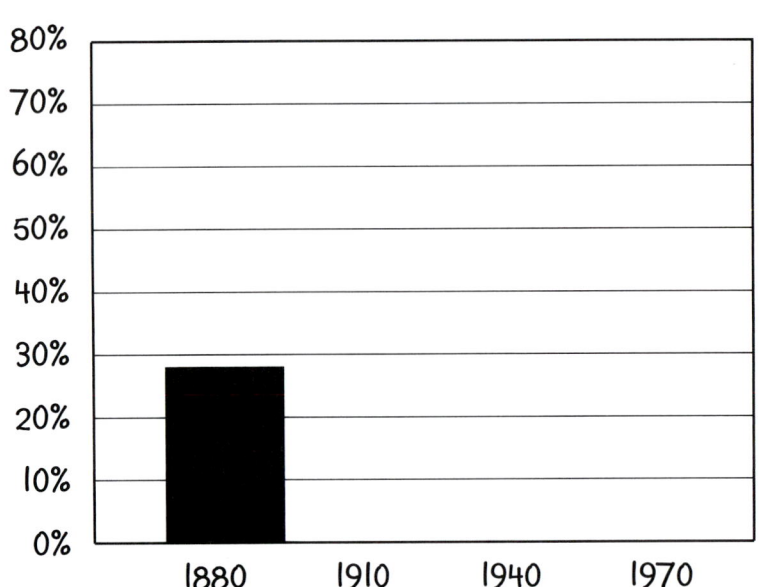

58 Level E • Lesson 5

SCIENCE

Climograph, Washington, D.C.

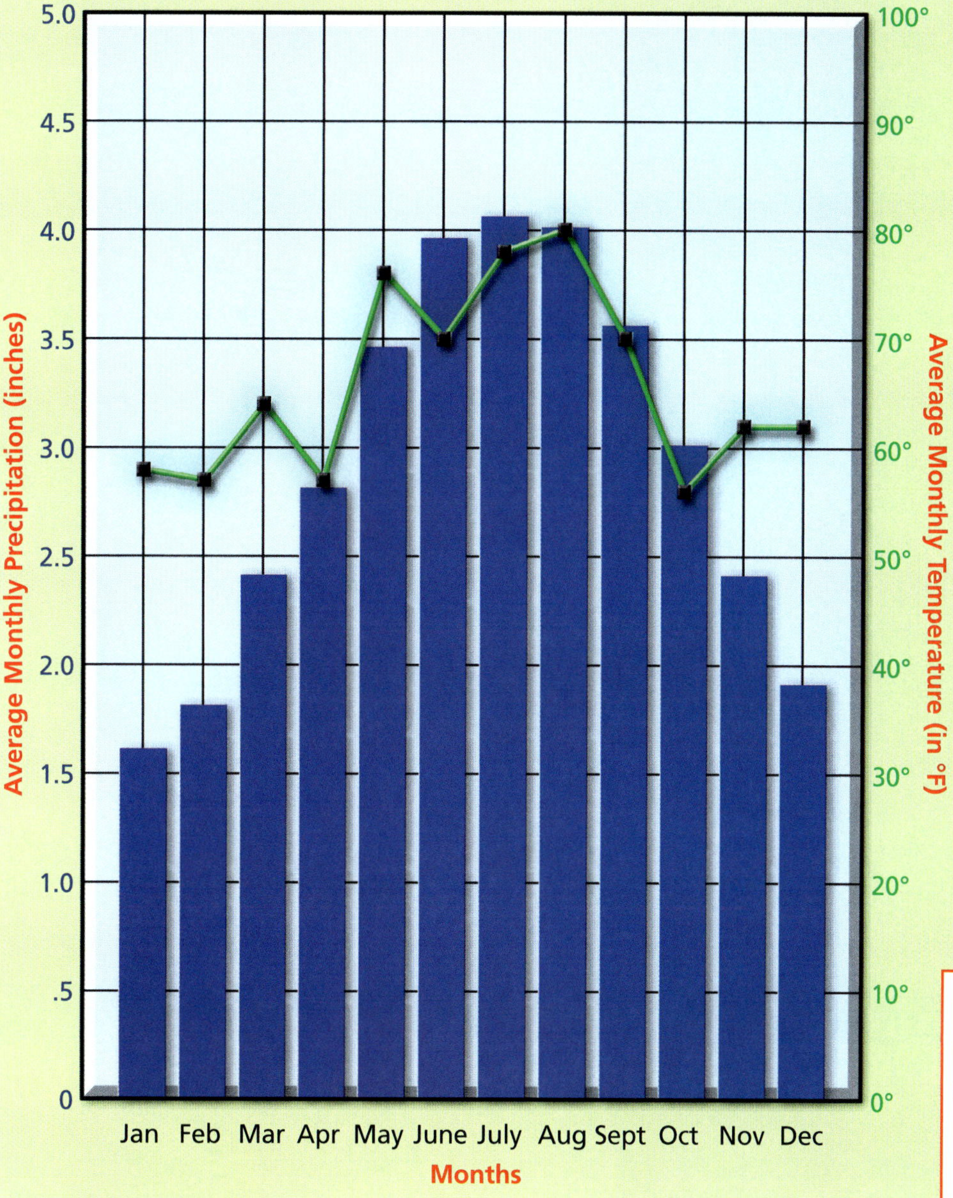

Understand Climographs

A **climograph** combines a bar graph and a line graph to show the average monthly temperature and average monthly precipitation for a place. **Precipitation** (pri-sip-uh-TAY-shuhn) is water falling from the sky in the form of rain, sleet, hail, or snow.

The climograph shows the average monthly rainfall (line) and temperature (bars) for Washington, D.C. Study the graph and answer the questions.

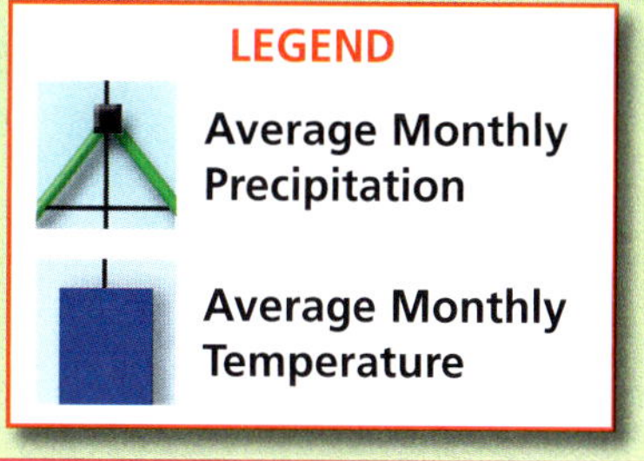

LEGEND

 Average Monthly Precipitation

 Average Monthly Temperature

WRITE HERE

1. What do the numbers on the left tell you?

2. What do the numbers on the right tell you?

3. Which is the warmest month in Washington, D.C.? (Look at the bars.)

4. Which is the coldest month?

5. How much rain falls in August?

6. Which season is the wettest?

Using Graphs and Charts   59

LESSON 5: Using Graphs and Charts

How a Bill Becomes a Law

Understand Flowcharts

A **flowchart** shows you the sequence, or order, of steps in a process. Flowcharts usually have arrows to show which step comes next. Always read the titles or labels that explain each step. Then follow the direction of the arrows. They tell you the correct sequence of the steps.

Idea for law

Bill is introduced in House or Senate

Bill is discussed in committees

House and Senate pass the bill

If the President agrees with the bill, he signs it

Bill becomes a law

WRITE HERE

Study the flowchart and answer the questions.

1. What is the subject of this flowchart?

2. What happens to the bill after it is introduced?

3. After the House and Senate pass the bill, where does it go?

Level E • Lesson 5

SOCIAL STUDIES

Make a Flowchart

Some decisions are easier to make than others. What movie or DVD game should you rent? That's not a very hard decision to make. Other decisions are harder. You may have to vote for a class president. Which candidate is better? Imagine that your school might vote on adding more recycling areas around your school. Is it a good idea? How do you decide?

Problem-solving and decision-making skills help you make better choices. These skills use steps. 1.) You must identify the problem. 2.) You need to gather information about the problem. 3.) Study the information you have gathered. It may tell you something about solving the problem. 4.) Think about options, or choices. Think of as many ways as you can to solve the problem. 5.) Choose one of the solutions you think will best solve the problem. 6.) Take action. Make a plan to carry out your solution. 7.) Review the results of your solution. Does it work? Do you need to change your plan so that you get better results?

Turning this information into a flowchart will make it easier to understand. The first step is done for you.

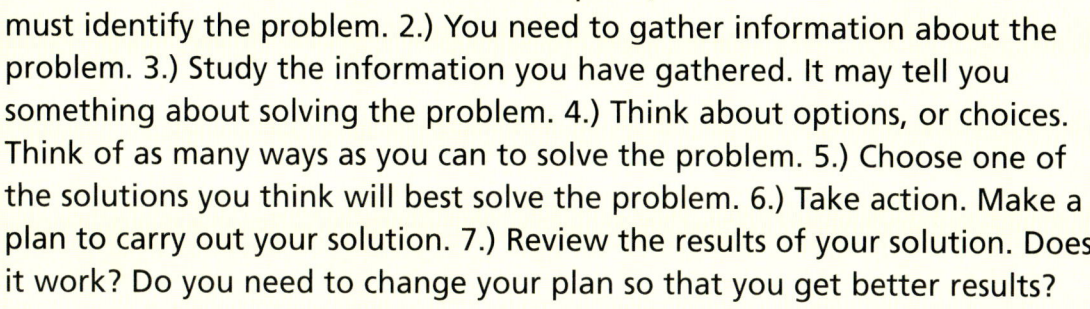

Solving Problems and Making Decisions

Identify the Problem

↓

_____

↓

_____

↓

_____

↓

_____

↓

_____

↓

_____

Using Graphs and Charts 61

LESSON 5

Using Graphs and Charts

Understand Circle Graphs

A **circle graph** shows you how a whole is divided into parts, called sectors. Circle graphs are also called **pie graphs** because the graph looks like a pie. Each sector, or slice of pie, is written as a percentage. These numbers in the circle graph add up to 100%. Remember that *whole* means 100%.

Study the legend. This box tells you what the colors stand for. In this graph, each type of energy use is shown in a different color.

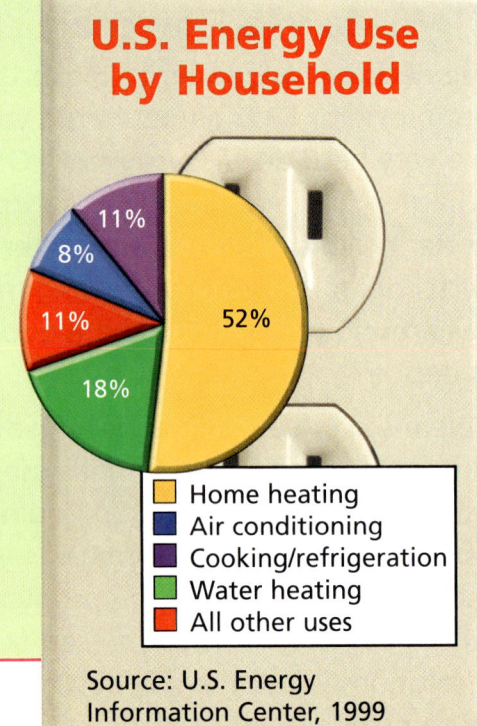

U.S. Energy Use by Household

- 11%
- 8%
- 11%
- 52%
- 18%

Legend:
- Home heating
- Air conditioning
- Cooking/refrigeration
- Water heating
- All other uses

Source: U.S. Energy Information Center, 1999

WRITE HERE

Study the circle graph and answer the questions.

1. Write the amount of energy used by each sector. Then add up all the sectors, or slices, in the circle graph.

   Home heating _____ %

   Air conditioning _____ %

   Cooking/refrigeration _____ %

   Water heating _____ %

   All other uses _____ %

   Total _____ %

2. What type of household purpose or function uses the most energy?

   _____

3. How much energy is used by a typical household for air conditioning?

   _____

4. Does home heating or water heating use more energy?

   _____

5. Think about the different things in your home that use energy. List four appliances in your home that might be included in "All other uses."

   _____

   _____

SOCIAL STUDIES

Understand Time Lines

A **time line** is a type of flowchart. It shows events in the order in which they happened. This type of graph helps you understand and remember the sequence, or time order, of events.

Always read the title of the time line. Then read the dates at the beginning and end of the time line. These dates tell the period of history that is covered.

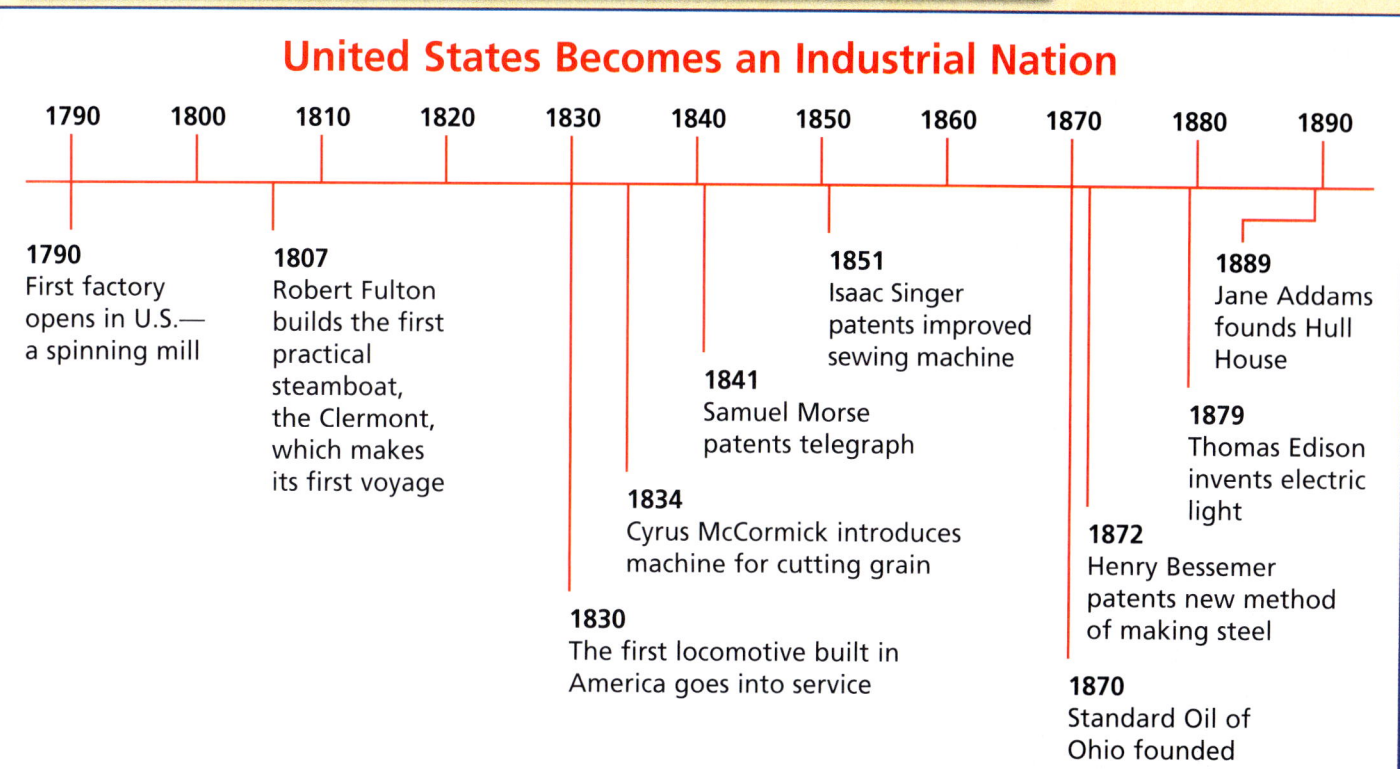

United States Becomes an Industrial Nation

- **1790** First factory opens in U.S.—a spinning mill
- **1807** Robert Fulton builds the first practical steamboat, the Clermont, which makes its first voyage
- **1830** The first locomotive built in America goes into service
- **1834** Cyrus McCormick introduces machine for cutting grain
- **1841** Samuel Morse patents telegraph
- **1851** Isaac Singer patents improved sewing machine
- **1870** Standard Oil of Ohio founded
- **1872** Henry Bessemer patents new method of making steel
- **1879** Thomas Edison invents electric light
- **1889** Jane Addams founds Hull House

WRITE HERE

Read the time line and answer the questions.

1. Read the title and the first and last date on the time line. What do you think this time line is about? Write another title for the time line.

2. How many years does this time line span?

3. How many years after the steamboat made its first voyage was the first locomotive built?

4. When did Samuel Morse patent the telegraph?

5. In 1879, Edison invented the electric light. How does this invention help you in your life today?

Using Graphs and Charts 63

LESSON 5
Using Graphs and Charts

Make a Time Line

Time lines can be horizontal (left to right) or vertical (top to bottom). Use the blank time line below to show events that happened in your life last week. Start the time line with last Monday. Then add the other days of the week. Add events that happened during the week. Did you go to a movie? Did you have a test or a quiz? A time line is a good way to keep track of events.

Day — **Event**

Monday

NET CONNECTION
Make your own charts and graphs at
http://www.smartdraw.com

GETTING READY

A Nation of Immigrants

In the years after the Civil War (1861–1865), America's population grew quickly. From 1870 to 1920, millions of immigrants came to America, looking for a new start in life.

LESSON 6

Think About Cause and Effect

Informational articles often explain events by using cause-and-effect relationships. A **cause** is the reason something happened. The **effect** is the result, or what happened. For example, *Because many immigrants could not find jobs in their homelands* (cause), *they came to the United States* (effect, or result).

Cause	Effect
Many immigrants could not find jobs in their homelands.	→ They came to the United States.

To find cause-and-effect relationships, follow these steps:

- Look for the **effect**, or result. Find *what happened* in your reading. Sometimes, clue words point to an effect. Look for words such as *therefore*, *as a result*, or *so*.

- Look for the **cause**. Ask *why* the event happened. Look for clue words that signal a cause: *because*, *caused*, or *since*. <mark>Because many immigrants could not find jobs in their homelands,</mark> they came to the United States. The cause = many immigrants could not find jobs in their homelands.

- Sometimes the effect comes before the cause.

Think About the Topic

What do you know about immigration to the United States? Quickly look through pages 65–76 of this article. Read the heads and look at the illustrations.

Now, reread the above introduction to "A Nation of Immigrants." Write two facts about immigration below.

1. _____

2. _____

Understanding Cause and Effect 65

LESSON 6: Understanding Cause and Effect

STRATEGIES•TEST PREP
- Question
- Understand Cause and Effect
- Make an Inference
- Compare and Contrast
- Tell Fact from Opinion
- Use Study Skills

Question

At different points in the article, stop and ask yourself: *Why did the author tell me this?* Look to see if the author uses cause-and-effect relationships.

Why does the author give information about Sweden? It helps you understand why Swedes came to America. They wanted to own their own land.

A Nation of Immigrants

Between 1870 and 1920, millions of people immigrated to America. They left Europe looking for a better life. Some came because they could not find jobs in their countries. Others could not buy land. For example, by 1870, the population of Sweden had doubled. Almost half the Swedes did not own land. They had to work on other people's farms for small wages. Many came to America looking for their own land.

Many immigrants came here to practice their religion or to gain political freedom. All these immigrants had one thing in common: They believed America held the promise of a new, better life.

America's industries were growing too. They needed more workers. Some states actually sent representatives to Europe to try to attract people to come to work in America. Private companies did the same thing. These companies put up posters showing how easy life was in America. Many of these claims were not true.

WRITE HERE

The author tells you that America's industries were growing. Does this help you understand why so many immigrants came to America? How does it help you?

_____

_____

_____

© 2003 Options Publishing Inc.

66 Level E • Lesson 6

Improvements in Transportation

Better forms of transportation helped make this wave of immigration to America's East Coast possible. By the 1870s, steam-driven ships replaced the slower sailing ships for the journey across the Atlantic Ocean. Now the journey from Europe to America took about fourteen days, instead of six weeks to six months.

From Europe to America

But the trip to America was still not easy. Most of the immigrants were poor. They could not afford to travel in luxury. As a result, passengers had to buy tickets in steerage. This part of the ship was below the deck. Steerage was originally designed for animals and freight below deck. It was dirty and overcrowded. There was no light and little room to move about. Because people were packed together so tightly, illnesses quickly spread. Many were seasick. These passengers did not breathe fresh air or see the open sky during the entire trip.

Immigrants crowd together on the deck of a ship.

Understand Cause and Effect

A **cause** is the reason something happened. The **effect** is the result, or what happened.

The **cause** is "people were packed together so tightly." What is the result? I'll read to see what happened. "Illnesses quickly spread."

WRITE HERE

Find one other cause-and-effect statement in the same paragraph.

Cause: _____

Effect: _____

Understanding Cause and Effect

LESSON 6: Understanding Cause and Effect

In 1901, seven-year-old Pauline Newman came by ship to America. She traveled with her mother and two sisters. She describes the trip as "cold, stormy, and uncomfortable. There were three layers of bunks, no fresh air, and it was crowded." They were given boiled water to drink. But if they did not have tea, they had to drink a cup of hot water. Sometimes, they were given a tasteless, watery soup.

Between 1870 and 1920, over 20 million people came to America. Many people came from southern and eastern Europe. These immigrants were mostly Italian, Jewish, and Polish. They arrived at Ellis Island, near New York City.

The immigrants that arrived in New York had to pass through Ellis Island, a small island outside of Manhattan. Doctors examined every immigrant. Most of the officials did not speak the immigrant's language. This was a frightening experience. If they did not pass the physical and written exams, they had to return to their homeland. Some immigrants waited as long as six weeks before their exams.

Use Cause and Effect to Make an Inference

An **inference** is a logical guess based on the details and information you are given. To make an inference, use the facts, your knowledge, and your common sense. Look for the causes and the effects.

Immigrants wait to be examined at Ellis Island.

WRITE HERE

Ellis Island was a frightening experience for many immigrants. If they failed the exam, they would have to go back to their homeland.

What other detail in the paragraph might add to an immigrant feeling afraid and confused?

Level E • Lesson 6

Many people lost all their belongings. Pauline Newman recalls that her family's luggage was lost at Ellis Island. Because they did not speak English, they could not get someone to help them find their suitcases. They lost everything: clothing, bedding, and pots and pans.

Life in America

Most of the immigrants did pass the exams. Some went to other parts of the United States, but many stayed in New York. Millions lived in the city because they were too poor to move to other areas of the country. By 1900, 3.5 million people lived in New York City. Of that total population, 1.3 million were born in another country. Pauline and her family found an apartment with two tiny rooms. The bedroom had no windows. The apartment had no bathroom.

As Pauline and others settled in New York, they found that life in America was very different from life in Europe. Most of them came from small villages. Many had their own house with a garden. Now they were in crowded apartment buildings called **tenements**. Most of these tenements had very little light or air. Often, as many as ten or twelve people lived in one room.

An immigrant family makes clothing in their tenement apartment.

SOCIAL STUDIES

tenement
(TEN-uh-muhnt)
a run-down apartment building, usually crowded and in a poor part of a city.

Compare and Contrast

For many immigrants, life in America was very different from life in Europe. Think about the **causes**, or reasons, that made their lives different. Remember, to **compare**, look at how things are the same. To **contrast**, look at how things are different.

WRITE HERE

List details that compare the differences between how some immigrants lived in Europe and how they lived in America.

Life in Europe

1. _____

2. _____

3. _____

Life in America

1. _____

2. _____

3. _____

Understanding Cause and Effect

Lesson 6: Understanding Cause and Effect

Use Primary Sources

A **primary source** is a record made by people who lived during an event. Old photographs, diaries and journals written at the time, and artwork are examples of primary sources. Look at the two images. One shows wealthy people gathering during the late 1800s. In 1889, Jacob Riis took the photo below. He was a Danish immigrant famous for his photographs of immigrants and their conditions. These people worked from their tenement for very low wages.

Wealthy people enjoy an outdoor lunch.

Parents and children work long hours in their tenement apartments.

Study the two images and answer the questions.

What do these two images tell you about the differences between the way the rich lived and the poor lived? Use details from the images.

The new immigrants found jobs wherever they could. Many of them, like young Pauline, worked in clothing factories. The hours were long and the work was hard. These factories, called **sweatshops**, were not very safe places to work.

Many immigrants could not find work in factories. They worked in their tenements, sewing clothes, making paper flowers, and sorting various kinds of goods. Whole families worked, even the youngest children. The pay was very low.

One of the only escapes from tenement life was the neighborhood. As the immigrants settled, neighborhoods began to grow where people mingled with their countrymen. They spoke their own languages and celebrated their own holidays. For many immigrants, their only fun was gathering with people from their old homelands.

Some of the immigrants sold goods or foods from pushcarts. The neighborhoods became a common meeting place. People bought what they needed and did not have to travel far from their houses. Even today, some of the neighborhood names, such as Little Italy and Chinatown, survive.

Fear and Anger on the West Coast

A smaller number of immigrants came from China and Japan. They arrived on the West Coast in San Francisco, California.

Most Asian immigrants arrived at Angel Island on the West Coast near San Francisco. It was very different from Ellis Island. Instead of trying to help people get into the country, officials at Angel Island made it as hard as possible to get in. Because many Americans living in San Francisco feared these new immigrants, some Americans tried to discourage them from settling here.

SOCIAL STUDIES

sweatshop
a factory where laborers work long hours under very poor conditions and very low wages.

Tell Fact from Opinion

To make good decisions about the information you read, you must be able to tell the difference between a fact and an opinion.

Facts can be proved to be true. Some facts can be checked in a book or by asking an expert.

Opinions are what someone thinks, feels, or believes. They are neither true nor false. To find opinions, look for words that describe how someone feels or thinks.

WRITE HERE

Write one fact and one opinion from this paragraph.

Fact	Opinion
_____	_____
_____	_____

Understanding Cause and Effect

LESSON 6: Understanding Cause and Effect

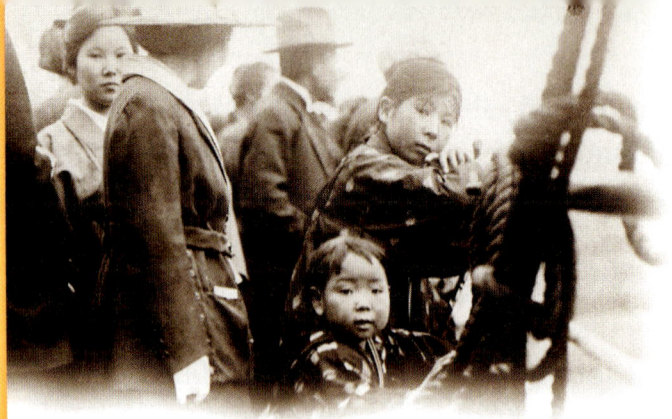

Japanese immigrants arrive at Angel Island off the California coast.

Look for Cause and Effect

Look for the **effect**, or result. Find *what happened* in the article. Look for clue words that point to an effect, such as *therefore*, *as a result*, or *so*.

Look for the **cause**. Ask *why* the event happened. Look for clue words that signal a cause, such as *because*, *caused*, or *since*.

Americans were afraid that the Chinese would steal their jobs (cause). As a result, Congress passed an act in 1882 called the Chinese Exclusion Act (effect, or result).

The Chinese and Japanese looked different from other immigrants. They dressed differently and had different customs. The Chinese worked very hard for low pay. **Americans were afraid that the Chinese would steal their jobs. As a result, Congress passed an act in 1882 called the Chinese Exclusion Act.** It barred Chinese workers from entering America. The purpose of Angel Island was to enforce this Act.

The Golden Door Closes

Many Americans thought immigrants would take their jobs and change the country. Their feelings toward immigrants and immigration changed. In 1917, during World War I, Americans became suspicious of immigrants.

In 1917, Congress passed a law that made immigrants prove they could read and write before they entered the country. Since many immigrants could not read or write, they were not allowed to enter the United States. In 1921, Congress passed other laws that limited the number of people who could come to the United States. America was closing its doors.

NET CONNECTION
http://www.tenement.org *and*
http://internationalchannel.com/education/ellis

WRITE HERE

Look for one more cause-and-effect relationship on this page. Write the cause and the effect below.

Cause   **Effect**

_____   _____

_____   _____

Level E • Lesson 6

Understand a Circle Graph

A **circle graph** shows how a whole is divided into parts, called sectors. Each sector is written as a percentage. The numbers in the circle graph add up to 100%. Remember that *whole* means 100%.

Between 1820 and 1925, more than 36 million people left their homelands for a new beginning in the United States. What countries did they come from?

Study the circle graph and answer the questions.

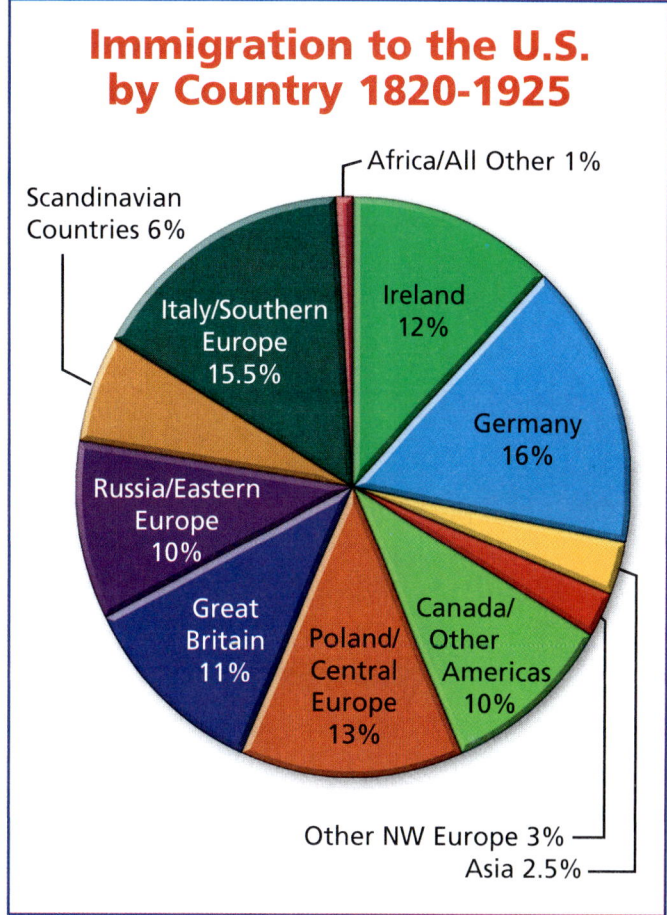

Immigration to the U.S. by Country 1820-1925

- Africa/All Other 1%
- Scandinavian Countries 6%
- Italy/Southern Europe 15.5%
- Ireland 12%
- Germany 16%
- Russia/Eastern Europe 10%
- Great Britain 11%
- Poland/Central Europe 13%
- Canada/Other Americas 10%
- Other NW Europe 3%
- Asia 2.5%

1. Between 1820 and 1925, which country represents the greatest number of immigrants to the United States?

   _____

2. Did more people come to America from Scandinavian countries or from Asian countries?

   _____

3. Circle the letter of the statement that is true about the makeup of the population of the United States between 1820 and 1925.

   a. Italy and the Southern European countries made up most of the immigrants to the United States.

   b. Immigrants from Africa made up the fewest number of immigrants to the United States.

Understanding Cause and Effect 73

LESSON 6: Understanding Cause and Effect

 ## Compare and Contrast Sources

Below is a primary source poster. In 1870, California published this poster to attract immigrants. Railroads and state governments printed fliers and posters to attract settlers to their regions. A *cornucopia* is a horn-shaped basket overflowing with fruit and grains. It is a symbol meaning "plenty." A **secondary source** is material or information about an earlier time or event written or made by people who lived at a later time. The article "A Nation of Immigrants" is a secondary source. It is a current article.

Primary Source from 1870

Secondary Source from this Article

Millions of immigrants were too poor to move to other areas of the country. By 1900, 3.5 million people lived in New York City. Of that number, 1.3 million were born in another country. Pauline and her family found an apartment with two tiny rooms. The bedroom had no windows. The apartment had no bathroom.

As Pauline and others settled in New York, they found that life in America was very different from life in Europe. Most of them came from small villages. Many had their own house with a garden. Now they were in crowded apartment buildings called tenements. Most of these tenements had very little light or air. Often, as many as ten or twelve people lived in one room.

Study the primary and secondary sources and answer the questions.

1. Do you think many immigrants were able to take advantage of the inexpensive land in California? Why or why not?

    _____
    _____

2. What do the two sources tell you about life in America during the late 1800s and early 1900s?

    _____
    _____

SOCIAL STUDIES

Recognize Cause and Effect

Remember that a **cause** is the reason something happened. The **effect** is the result, or what happened. Complete the cause-and-effect organizer below. Quickly look through, or skim, the article to find facts and details to help you make cause-and-effect statements. The organizer is started for you.

Cause: Why Something Happened	Effect: What Happened
Because many immigrants could not find jobs in their homelands,	they immigrated to the United States looking for a new start.
Since America's industries were growing quickly,	
	As a result, travelers had to buy tickets in steerage.
Because immigrants were packed together so tightly,	
	most passengers did not breathe fresh air or see the open sky for the entire trip.
Some immigrants arriving at Ellis Island did not pass the physical and written exams.	As a result,
Many immigrants lost their luggage. Because they did not speak English,	
Because many immigrants were too poor to move to other parts of the country,	
Because Asian immigrants looked different and had different customs,	

Understanding Cause and Effect

Understand Cause and Effect / Write a Persuasive Letter

A **persuasive letter** tries to convince readers to see your point of view. Imagine that it is 1902, and you write a letter to the newspaper. You want to convince readers that the journey by ship from Europe to America is very difficult and dangerous for immigrants. Suggest ways to make it better. You also want to convince your readers that Ellis Island needs translators, people who can speak English as well as another foreign language. Remember, the more examples you use the more persuasive your letter will be. Use cause-and-effect relationships to express your points. You may want to use some of the cause-and-effect statements you wrote on the graphic organizer on page 75.

_____

_____

_____

_____

_____

_____

_____

GETTING READY

LESSON 7

Energy: From the Wheel to the Stars

People have always looked for a better, faster way to travel. Whether to trade with new lands, explore the world around them, or travel from city to city, people want to get there faster. Many scientific inventions have changed the way we travel. From wheels to sails to steam to jets, our need to explore the world has created a revolution in travel.

Think About Classifying

When you **classify**, you group items or ideas together that have something in common. By classifying items, you organize information so that it can be easily understood or studied. An example of information grouped by categories is the classified section of the newspaper. If you looked under the category, or group, called *Automobiles*, you would see that this category is classified into subgroups: *Used Cars* and *New Cars*. Another example might be when you go to rent a movie. The store is grouped into two sections: videos and DVDs. You classify things every day. When you hear a song on the radio, you classify it as country, rock, rap, or disco. To classify information, follow these steps:

- Carefully examine the items. Think about what they have in common.
- Compare and contrast the items. How are they alike? How are they different?
- Then choose a characteristic that they have in common.

Think About the Topic

Reread the short introduction above for "Energy: From the Wheel to the Stars." Think about ways that people traveled using wind and animal power. Use your knowledge to classify types of transportation. Ask yourself: *What do I already know about how wind and animals were used for transportation?* Write two things you know under the categories below.

Wind Power

_____

_____

Animal Power

_____

_____

You just made your first classification. Classifying is important because it helps you organize and understand information.

Classifying 77

LESSON 7: Classifying

Energy: From the Wheel to the Stars

STRATEGIES • TEST PREP
- Question
- Classify
- Identify Main Idea/Supporting Details
- Draw Conclusions
- Use Study Skills

Question

Ask yourself questions when you read articles that give information. Change each heading into a question using *Who*, *What*, *When*, *Where*, *Why*, and *How*. This helps you classify information as you read.

The first heading becomes:

Who was on the move? People were on the move.

On the Move

From ancient times, early cultures have needed to travel, trade, and explore. At first, they wandered on foot. Then, thousands of years ago, humans tamed the wild horse. Now travelers could ride rather than walk. Horses improved travel. People also used them to plow the soil and plant crops.

Many historians believe that a civilization in Mesopotamia (me-suh-puh-TAY-mee-uh) invented the wheel in about 4000 B.C. Mesopotamia is an area between the Tigris and Euphrates rivers in present-day Iraq. With the invention of the wheel, it became possible for people to transport their crops from one place to another. They could now trade their crops for other goods.

Travel became more important. Carpenters built carts and chariots. About 3500 B.C., a wheeled vehicle called the chariot was built. The two-wheeled chariot, pulled by a horse, increased the speed of travel. This invention eventually led to four-wheeled carts.

As people traveled farther from their homes, their curiosity about the world around them increased. But there were problems with this method of transportation. When animals became sick or tired, travel stopped. They were not reliable for long-distance travel.

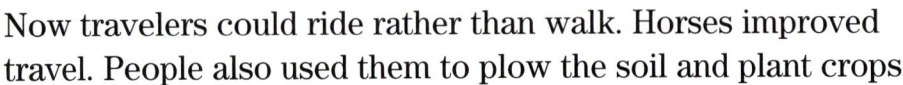

WRITE HERE

Read "On the Move." List two ways that early cultures used animals in their everyday lives.

1. _____

2. _____

Sails Make a Difference

Travel over water also improved. Early cultures, living next to water, used dug-out logs as boats. Travelers used wooden paddles to move these "dugouts" through the water. Boats began to move people and supplies across water.

Soon shipbuilders added sails to boats to harness the power of the wind. When the wind blew, boats moved more swiftly through the water.

Sailing ships increased **migration** and trade. From about 1200 to 350 B.C., the greatest traders of the ancient world were the Phoenicians (fi-NEE-shuhnz). They lived along the eastern coast of the Mediterranean Sea. Their ship, called a galley, had one large sail and several sets of oars. These seafarers traveled all over the Mediterranean, establishing colonies and trading posts.

As sailing ships improved, travelers journeyed farther from home. They brought back wonderful treasures. New markets for items such as silk and spices opened up new trade routes.

The map shows the main Phoenician trade routes. The Phoenicians were the most important trading nation in the Mediterranean.

migration
to move from one place to another.

sail
a large sheet of strong cloth that makes boats or ships move when it catches the wind.

Understand Classifying

When you **classify**, you group things together that have something in common. Classifying helps you understand and remember information.

WRITE HERE

1. List two kinds of boats used by early people to travel in or through water.

2. How did the Phoenicians make their galleys faster than the dugout?

Classifying 79

LESSON 7 Classifying

Classify Using a Diagram

A **diagram** is a drawing or a plan that explains or illustrates information.

The diagram on the next page shows the different parts of the *Mayflower*. The ship was only 108 feet long and carried 102 passengers and 18 crew members. The voyage took 66 days from England to present-day Massachusetts. Study the diagram and the information about the ship. Then answer the questions.

Phoenician galleys were sturdy ships built for exploration and trade.

Ships Lead The Age of Exploration

During the 1400s and 1500s, explorers from Portugal, Spain, England, and France set out in small ships to seek faster trade routes to Asia. These explorers discovered new lands and new routes for trade.

In the 1600s, when colonists sailed to the New World, their ships called galleons were too small and slow for their needs. Galleons carried heavy cannons for protection. They had several decks for passengers, livestock, crew, and cargo. The *Mayflower*, which carried 102 passengers, livestock, and supplies, was only 108 feet long. There was little room for passengers and cargo. The journeys were long and uncomfortable.

WRITE HERE

1. Look at the diagram on page 81. List the parts of the ship that were used for living areas by the captain, officers, crew, and passengers.

   _____

2. List two pieces of equipment used to perform work on the ship.

   _____

Parts of the Mayflower

A. The **round house** kept the ship's maps and charts.
B. The **ship's bell** marked the time of the watch and signaled emergencies.
C. The captain lived in the **great cabin**.
D. The **whipstaff** was a long lever that steered the ship.
E. The ship's officers lived in **steerage**.
F. The **capstan** was a pulley that hoisted cargo on deck.
G. The crew lived in the **forecastle**.
H. The passengers and livestock lived **between decks**.
I. The **gun room** kept two cannons for protection.
J. The **hold** stored most of the cargo, food, and supplies.
K. The **windlass** raised and lowered the anchors.

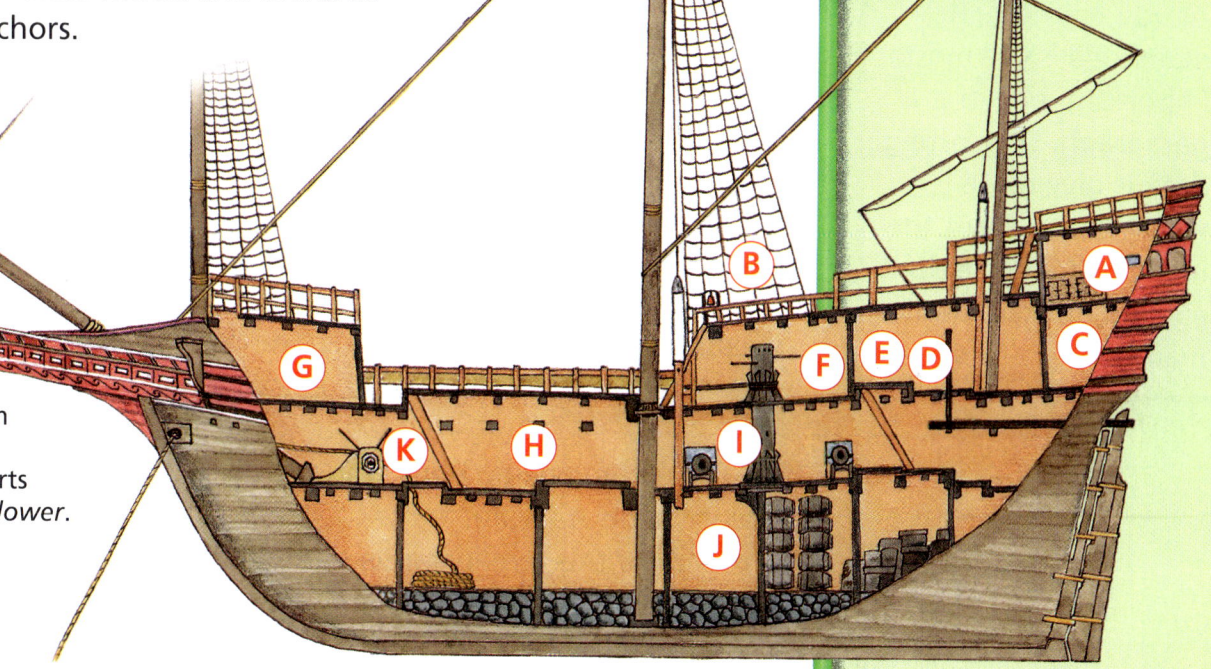

This diagram shows the different parts of the *Mayflower*.

WRITE HERE

3. List two areas for storage on the *Mayflower*.

___

4. Why do you think the ship was not comfortable for the passengers during the voyage to the New World? Use your knowledge and information from the article and the diagram.

___

Classifying 81

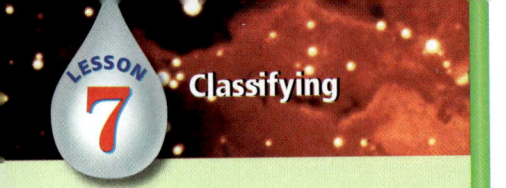

Lesson 7 Classifying

Classify Using Supporting Details

To understand what you read, you must look for the main idea. As you learned, the **main idea** is the most important idea in a paragraph. **Supporting details** give more information about the main idea. They help explain or examine the main idea.

The Golden Age of Sail

In the 1800s, the design of ships changed to improve speed and save costs. Schooners had smaller and fewer sails. They turned easily in the wind and could sail close to the coastline. They didn't need as many crew members. Brigs and barques (barks) used many large, square sails. These sails helped the crew move in strong ocean winds and currents. The ships were built for long ocean voyages. Clipper ships were built for speed. They were long, sleek, and the fastest ships of the time. They earned their name because they "clipped" several days from normal travel times.

The need for faster ships continued. In 1849, gold was discovered in California. Thousands of people caught "gold fever." They looked for a fast way to get to California. Advertisements stressed that clipper ships were the fastest means of travel. However, if there was no wind or if storms destroyed the sails, these ships slowed down or stopped. The journey might take three or four months. Even the fast clipper ships were not reliable transportation.

In Great Britain, new ideas and inventions began to change industry and, eventually, transportation. Inventors experimented with steam as an energy source. As long ago as 1769, a man from Scotland named James Watt invented a steam engine that would change the way people traveled.

The Age of Steam

The steam engine boils water to turn it into a gas called water vapor. As water turns to steam, it expands. The force or pressure of this expansion is the basis of all steam engines. Steam power drove machinery.

WRITE HERE

The main idea of this paragraph says that changes to the design of ships improved speed and saved costs. Read the paragraph and answer the question:

How did the shipbuilders improve speed and save money with the schooner and the barque?

From this invention, steamships became popular. They did not rely on wind, and they changed the way people and goods moved throughout the world. Steamships burned coal or wood to heat the water. The pressure from the steam ran **pistons**, which moved the ship. Before steamships, transatlantic voyages took between 70 and 120 days, depending on the weather. On April 8, 1838, the British steamship *Great Western* sailed from Bristol, England, and arrived in New York harbor in only 16 days.

The steam engine also improved travel over land. In 1825, the first steam railroad opened in England. It pulled 34 railcars. People and goods had never traveled so quickly.

In the United States in 1869, the Union Pacific Railroad was completed. No longer did people need wagon trains to make the long, dangerous trip across America. Travelers could now journey from the Atlantic Ocean to the Pacific Ocean by train.

The first steam engine invented by James Watt.

Science continues to change transportation. We started with the wheel and moved on to jet engines and rockets. We have escaped the pull of gravity and landed on the moon. From the wheel to the stars, science continues to change how and where we travel.

NET CONNECTION
http://www.si.edu/resource/faq/nmah/transportation.htm

SCIENCE

piston
a disk or cylinder connected to a rod that moves back and forth.

Classify to Draw a Conclusion

Before you can **draw conclusions**, you must understand the facts and information in an article. Find the facts in the first paragraph to complete the chart below.

WRITE HERE

Days for Ocean Trip Before Steamship	Days for Ocean Trip After Steamship

What conclusion can you draw from the supporting details in the chart?

Classifying

LESSON 7 Classifying

How to Classify Information

Charts help you classify information. Study the list of words about transportation below. They are names that appear in this lesson. Look through the article and classify them by the type of transportation they provide: land or water. Fill in the columns to complete the chart.

Great Western	schooner	cart
Mayflower	chariot	clipper
dugout	railroad	galley
wagon trains	brigs	barques
horse	Union Pacific	wheel

Land Transportation

_____
_____
_____
_____
_____
_____
_____
_____
_____
_____

Water Transportation

_____
_____
_____
_____
_____
_____
_____
_____
_____
_____

Understand Latitude and Longitude
Science on the Seas

As people moved around the world, they needed a way to understand and classify the seas. Navigators know their exact position on the earth's surface by using a system of imaginary lines called *latitude* and *longitude*. Lines of latitude circle the earth horizontally, starting at the equator (0°). Other lines of latitude are given a value for how many degrees north or south they are from the equator.

Lines of longitude circle the earth vertically. They pass through the North and South Poles. The main line of longitude is the Greenwich Meridian, or prime meridian. It also has a value of 0°. All other lines of longitude are given values for how many degrees they are to the west or the east of the prime meridian. Degrees of longitude meet at the poles and are farthest apart at the equator.

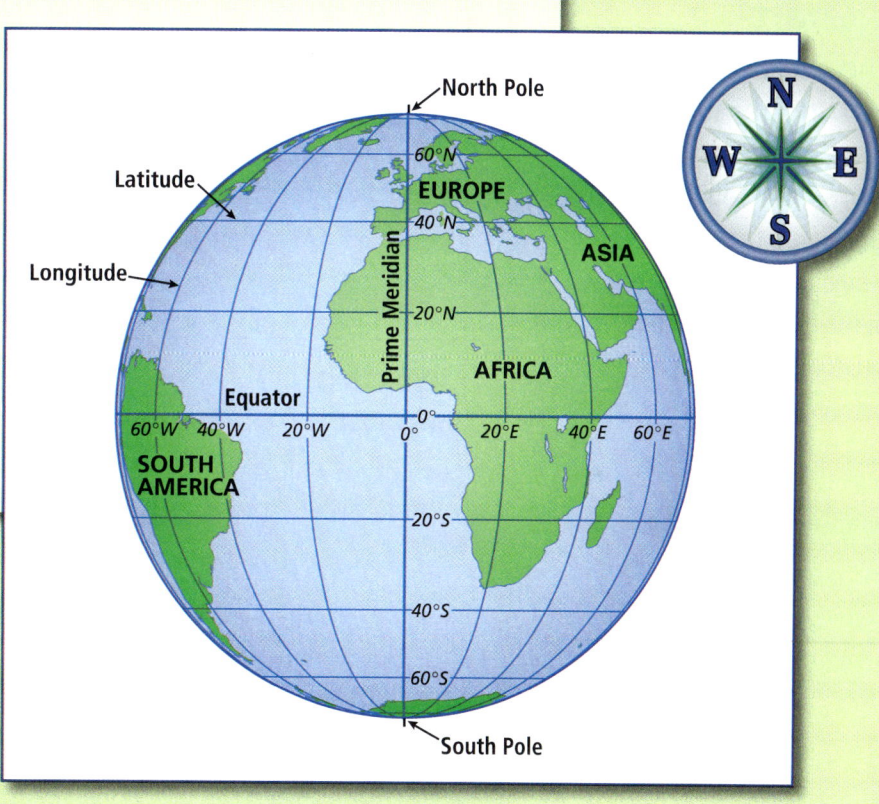

WRITE HERE

Study the diagram of the world and the lines of **latitude** and **longitude**. Circle the answer that completes each sentence.

1. Lines of latitude circle the earth **(horizontally) (vertically)**.
2. Lines of longitude circle the earth **(horizontally) (vertically)**.
3. The equator is a line of **(latitude) (longitude)**.
4. The prime meridian is a line of **(latitude) (longitude)**.

LESSON 7: Classifying

Increase of Railroad Tracks in Europe from 1840 to 1860

	1840*	1860*
Austria-Hungary	144 km	4,543 km
Belgium	334 km	1,730 km
France	496 km	9,167 km
Germany	469 km	11,089 km
Great Britain	2,390 km	14,603 km
Italy	20 km	2,404 km
Netherlands	17 km	335 km
Russia	27 km	1,626 km
Spain	—	1,917 km
Sweden	—	527 km

*Length of rail tracks in kilometers. Note: 1km = 5/8 mile.
Source: Fordham University Internet Modern History Sourcebook

Classify Using a Chart

The **chart** shows the growth of railroads in ten European countries from 1840 to 1860. It classifies the development of railways by country. Study the chart and answer the questions.

WRITE HERE

1. Which country had the most kilometers of railroad track in 1840? _____

   In 1860? _____

2. Name one country that began laying railroad tracks after 1840.

   _____

3. Which country had the greatest increase of railroad tracks between 1840 and 1860? Show your work.

   _____

   _____

86 Level E • Lesson 7

Understand an Illustration

The illustration below is titled "How a Steam Locomotive Works." A firebox at the back of the locomotive burns **coal** or **wood**. The **combustion**, or burning, of fuel makes water boil inside pipes. The water changes into **steam** and expands. The pressure from the steam drives pistons back and forth. The pistons are connected to rods called **crankshafts**. When the crankshaft rotates, it turns the locomotive's wheels.

Read the title and all the labels. Study the illustration and answer the questions.

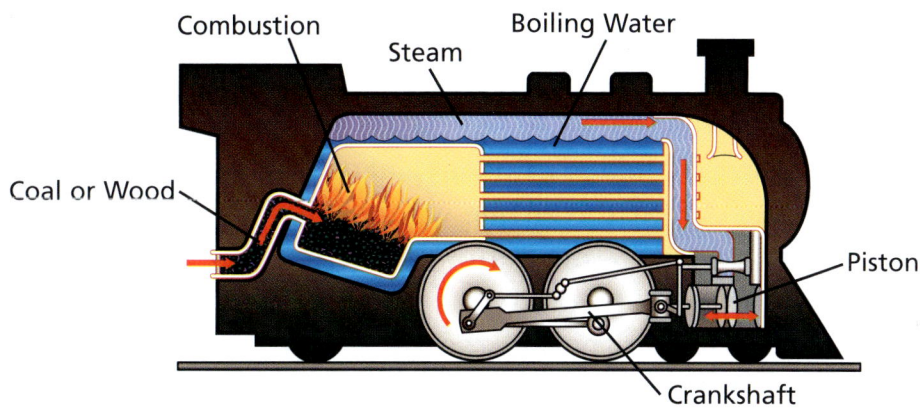

How a Steam Locomotive Works

1. Why is coal or wood important to how the steam engine works?

   _____

2. What process causes water to change into steam? _____

3. Based on the information in the illustration, number the five events below in the order in which they occur. The first one is done for you.

   _____ pistons move back and forth

   __1__ firebox burns coal

   _____ crankshaft rotates, or turns, the wheels

   _____ train moves

   _____ water changes to steam

Classifying 87

LESSON 7 Classifying

Write a Description

Read the interview of Charles Hardee written in 1928. He describes an early train trip.

"In 1844, I was sent to old Franklin College in Athens, Georgia. I was 14 years old. At Augusta, [Georgia], I took the Georgia Railroad to Union Point, which was 90 miles away. From Union Point, I went to Athens by way of a branch rail line, which was 40 miles long, and recently built.

Five nights a week, the passenger service on this road was by horsecar. It was an all night trip, and not a very comfortable one. There was a long bench running the whole length of the car on each side. On the sixth night, the horsecar was hitched to a freight train that had a baggage car and a freight car. All the cars were then attached to a small steam engine called 'The Fire Fly.'

At one very steep hill, the train would stop and the engine would be fired up. When it was thought that the engine had enough steam to climb over the top of the grade, it would start off to make the climb. Often, before the train reached the top, the engine would stop for lack of steam power. It would roll back down to the bottom of the hill to the starting point, and be fired again. This procedure was sometimes repeated three or four times before the 'Fire Fly' went over the top."

Adapted from the Library of Congress, American Life Histories: Federal Writer's Project, 1936–1940.

Imagine that it is 1850. You have just taken a trip on a steam train. Write a brief description of your trip and how the train's steam engine works. You may look back at the article to help you explain the process used in train steam engines.

_____
_____
_____
_____
_____

GETTING READY

Give Us Freedom

In late August of 1839, a long, low ship sailed into Culloden Point off Long Island, New York. The ship was named *Amistad*, which in Spanish means "friendship." The Africans aboard the *Amistad* were scared and hungry. Their future was uncertain. Would they ever return home to Africa? What happened on the *Amistad* and to the Africans and their leader, Sengbe Pieh, *(sing-BAY PEE-ay)* greatly changed America's view on slavery.

Think About Fact and Opinion

In the early 1800s, it was illegal to bring in new people as slaves to America and Cuba. But laws did not stop the slave trade. This historic story about the *Amistad* captives is an informational article. It contains both facts and opinions. As you read, you make decisions about the information you are given. To make good decisions, you must be able to tell the difference between a fact and an opinion. Good decisions are based on facts.

- A **fact** is something that is true. *Sengbe was on the* Amistad. You can prove this is a fact by looking in a history book or encyclopedia.

- An **opinion** is what someone thinks, feels, or believes. Opinions are neither true nor false. They cannot be proved. *Sengbe loved his village.* The word *loved* tells you this is a feeling, and feelings are opinions.

Think About the Topic

Reread the short introduction above for "Give Us Freedom." Write two facts that you learned about the *Amistad* on the lines below.

1. _____

_____

_____

_____

_____

2. _____

_____

_____

_____

_____

Telling Fact from Opinion

LESSON 8
Telling Fact from Opinion

STRATEGIES • TEST PREP
- Question
- Tell Fact from Opinion
- Use Context Clues
- Make an Inference
- Draw Conclusions
- Use Study Skills

barracoon
(bar-uh-KOON) a prison made of sturdy wooden poles clamped together by iron bars with a roof made of wood and covered with grass.

Question
Every paragraph contains a main, or most important, idea. As you read, ask yourself: *What is the most important idea in this paragraph?*

Give Us Freedom

A Man Called Sengbe

Sengbe Pieh (sing-BAY PEE-ay) often walked from his home to his rice fields alone. He lived in the village of Mani in the country known as Mende in West Africa. It was quiet and peaceful. But in 1839, neighboring nations were at war. Sengbe knew that danger might reach his village.

Early one January morning, Sengbe headed to his rice fields. He left his wife, three children, and his father at home. Suddenly, on the road in front of him he saw four men. They quickly surrounded Sengbe and threw him to the ground. Despite Sengbe's strength, he could not escape the kidnappers. They tied his right hand tightly to his neck and led him away from Mani. They marched him through forests and swamps. Then Sengbe was taken to Lomboko Island.

Sengbe watched as more and more captives arrived on Lomboko. Like him, the men, women, and children were chained and packed into prisons called **barracoons**. A slave dealer named Pedro Blanco owned the prisons. When Sengbe's barracoon held about six hundred people, Blanco checked them over. He looked at their eyes and teeth. He also made them jump to see if they were strong. He did not want to buy any sick or weak slaves. Sengbe was an easy purchase. He was a healthy, strong man in his mid-twenties.

✏️ **WRITE HERE**

What is the main idea of the second paragraph?

_____
_____
_____

90 Level E • Lesson 8

The Voyage to Cuba

In darkness the captives were loaded onto a large slave ship named the *Tecora* and pushed below deck. The ceiling of the hold was so low that the Africans could not stand up. They sat chained side by side. The cramped conditions were unbearable. During their three-month journey to Cuba, the slaves left the hold only once a day. The captives felt angry and confused. They were given little food, water, or fresh air. Many captives died. Others were beaten.

In June of 1839, the *Tecora* finally arrived in Havana. The slavers marched the captives through the streets at night and locked them up in a barracoon. Days later, Sengbe and 52 others were sold to two Spaniards. Jose Ruiz, a plantation owner, and Pedro Montes also bought papers that gave each slave a Spanish name. Then they took their slaves to a fast, black **schooner**, the *Amistad*. The slaves were forced on board and down into the hold. The ship left port and headed for Puerto Principe, Cuba.

A barracoon, or prison, like the one owned by Pedro Blanco.

SOCIAL STUDIES

schooner (SKOO-nur) a fast sailing ship.

Tell Fact from Opinion

As you read, look for facts and opinions. This helps you make decisions and draw the correct conclusions about what you read. **Facts** are true. They can be proved. **Opinions** are what someone thinks, feels, or believes. They are neither true nor false. To find opinions, look for words that describe how someone feels.

WRITE HERE

On the lines below, write two facts and two opinions from the first paragraph.

Facts

1. _____
2. _____

Opinions

1. _____
2. _____

Telling Fact from Opinion

Lesson 8: Telling Fact from Opinion

shackles
(SHAK-uhlz) heavy iron chain that locks around the ankles.

Use Context Clues

Sometimes, authors give you clues to the meaning of a new word by defining the word for you. A **definition clue** tells you the meaning of the new word by defining it or by stating it in a slightly different way.

Sengbe sat chained in the dark, dreary hold and listened to people crying. Sengbe desperately wanted to escape. He studied the crew and asked the other slaves to tell him what they could see. The slaves also looked around the hold for tools or weapons. By luck, they found a sharp nail that would open their **shackles**. That night Sengbe unlocked his chains first. One by one the other captives were freed.

Next, the Africans tore open a crate full of knives and passed them around. Sengbe waited until the crew was asleep before he took charge. He led the Africans on deck, where they quickly killed the captain and the cook. Two crew members escaped in a small lifeboat. That left Ruiz and Montes, whom Sengbe did not want to kill. He knew he would need them to steer the ship. Sengbe ordered the Spaniards to turn the *Amistad* eastward, toward Africa. Little did Sengbe and the others know that by night, Montes turned the ship westward.

A Difficult Voyage

For two months, the *Amistad* zigzagged its way up the east coast of the United States. By moving the ship in short, sharp turns, Montes confused Sengbe. They passed several ships along the way. The captains on these ships thought the *Amistad* was strange-looking. Was it a pirate ship? But by now Sengbe knew what Montes had done. He also knew that the Africans needed more food and water. Some slaves had already died and many were sick.

WRITE HERE

Read these sentences from the article. Write the definition clue the author uses to help you understand what the word *zigzagged* means.

For two months, the *Amistad* zigzagged its way up the east coast of the United States. By moving the ship in short, sharp turns, Montes confused Sengbe.

_____

_____

SOCIAL STUDIES

Find Facts in a Map

This map shows the voyages of the *Tecora* and *Amistad* in 1839. It also shows you the route of the ship the *Gentleman*, on which Sengbe and the others returned to Africa after the trial. Look for Lomboko Island and where Sengbe Pieh lived in Mende, also called Mendeland.

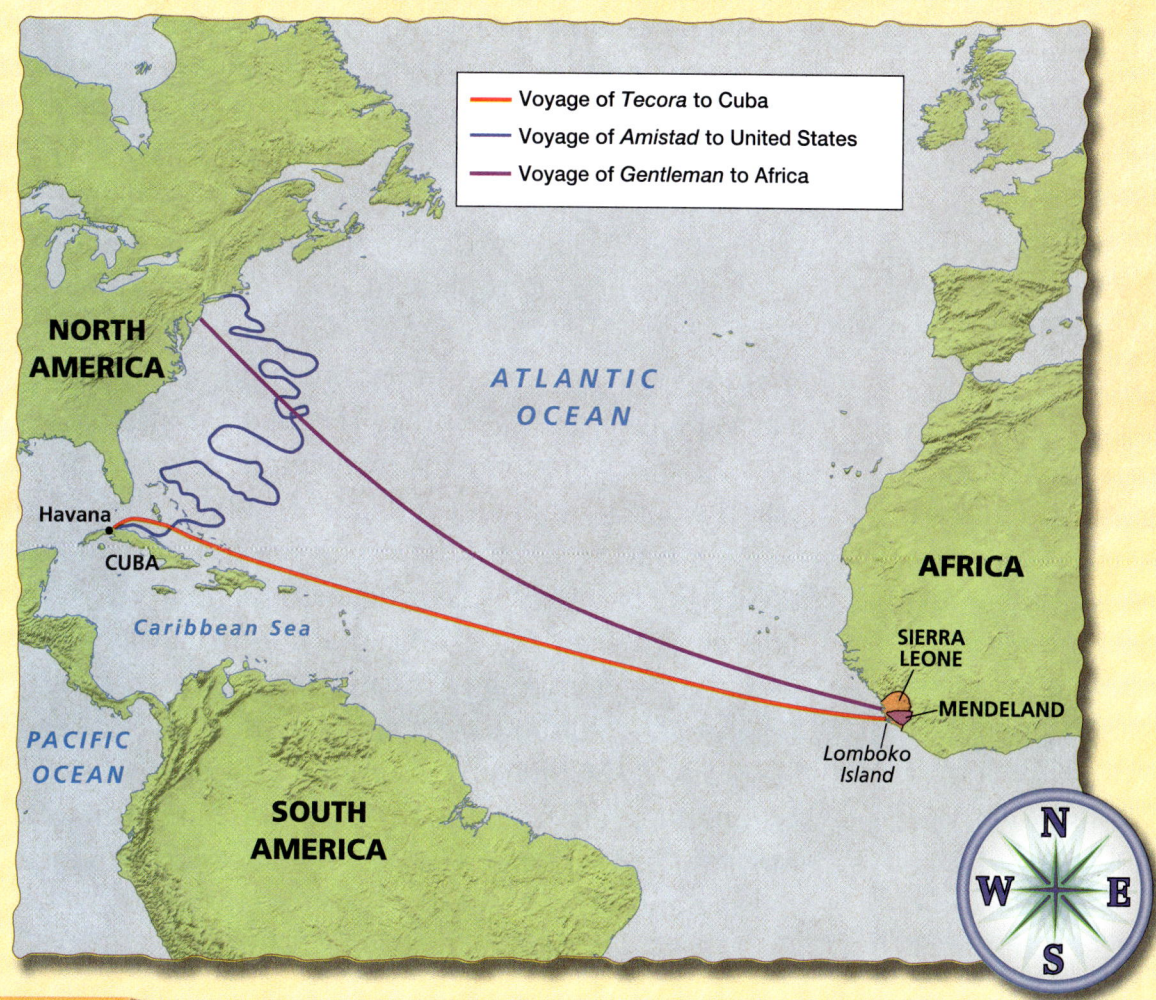

WRITE HERE

1. In what direction did the *Tecora* travel from Africa? Next, describe the direction or route the *Amistad* followed after it left Cuba.

2. In your opinion, should the *Amistad* captives have tried to sail back to Africa? Give reasons to support your answer.

Telling Fact from Opinion 93

LESSON 8: Telling Fact from Opinion

abolitionists
(ab-uh-LISH-uh-nists) people who fought against slavery.

piracy
(PYE-ruh-see) robbery on the high seas.

Use Facts to Make an Inference

When you **make an inference**, you make a logical guess based on the information and facts you are given. For example, you see dark clouds and hear thunder. Using your knowledge, you can infer (guess) that a storm is coming.

In August, when the ship reached Long Island, New York, it dropped anchor. Sengbe rowed ashore with some men to trade the ship's goods and coins for food. Meanwhile, the U.S.S. *Washington* was on patrol. It spotted the "mysterious" ship and drew closer.

The *Amistad* is Found

Lieutenant Commander Thomas Gedney had never seen an all-black crew on a schooner the size of the *Amistad*. He sensed something was wrong. The ship's sails were torn. Also, the outside of the ship was in poor shape. Gedney boarded the *Amistad*. His sailors found Montes and Ruiz hidden in the hold. The men told Gedney about the rebellion. They said "a man named Cinque" was the slaves' leader. Sengbe and the others were found on shore and returned to the ship.

Under orders, Gedney took control of the *Amistad*. His ship towed it to New London, Connecticut. News about the *Amistad* swirled across the nation. Southerners wanted the slaves punished because they rebelled. **Abolitionists** believed the Africans were innocent and should be freed. Some thought that the Africans should go back to Cuba.

At a hearing aboard the *Washington*, Ruiz and Montes told their story to a judge. They claimed their captives were *Ladinos*, African slaves born in Cuba. This was an important point because bringing Africans into Cuba was illegal. Ruiz and Montes showed the papers that said the slaves were legal. They asked the judge to return the slaves and their ship. Without hearing from the Africans, the judge freed Ruiz and Montes. The Africans were jailed and ordered to face trial for murder and **piracy**.

WRITE HERE

1. What inferences can you make about the slave dealers Ruiz and Montes?

2. What can you infer about the judge's decision?

A scene from the trial painted by Hale Woodruff during the 1930s.

The Trial

A team of abolitionists raised money to help the Africans. They hired lawyers for them. They also found someone who spoke the Africans' language. At the jail, hundreds of people lined up to see the *Amistad* captives. They were curious because they had heard stories about "man-eaters" and murderers. They found the Africans to be smart, decent people. Public sympathy grew.

In September of 1839, a judge ruled that the Africans could not be tried for murder or piracy. He said the alleged crimes happened on a Spanish ship and in Spanish waters. So, the case was moved to higher court.

In January, hearings began in district court. Lawyers for Ruiz and Montes claimed that the Africans were legally slaves. Lawyers for the Africans disagreed. The lawyers said that the captives were farmers, blacksmiths, and warriors who had been kidnapped from Africa.

Use Facts to Draw a Conclusion

Sometimes an author does not tell you everything in what you read. You need to draw your own conclusion from the facts the author gives you. To **draw a conclusion**, you make a judgment based only on the facts presented.

WRITE HERE

Think about what you have read so far of "Give Us Freedom." What conclusions can you make about Sengbe Pieh? Be sure to look back at what you have read to find facts that support your conclusion.

_____
_____
_____

LESSON 8: Telling Fact from Opinion

appeal (uh PEEL) to ask for a decision made by a court of law to be changed.

Sengbe, a proud and smart man, testified. He talked about his treatment as a slave. His speech was moving. When he finished, he cried out in English, "Give us free!" Judge Andrew Judson ruled in favor of the Africans.

The case was **appealed** to the United States Supreme Court. Former President John Quincy Adams led the defense. He pleaded with the court to set the Africans free.

Finally, in March of 1841, the Supreme Court upheld, or agreed with, the decision that the lower court had made. After two long years, the Africans won their freedom.

Sengbe and the other *Amistad* captives returned to Africa in November of 1841. They sailed back to Africa on a ship called the *Gentleman*. Their long journey back home was over.

A portrait of John Quincy Adams, painted by George Peter Alexander Healy in 1858.

Identify Fact and Opinion

Facts tell you what a person thinks, feels, or believes. When you read that Sengbe was proud and smart, or that his speech was moving, you are reading the author's opinions. They add interest to the article, but they do not give you facts.

NET CONNECTION
http://www.amistad.mysticseaport.org

WRITE HERE

Why do you think it is important to be able to tell the difference between a fact and an opinion?

_____
_____
_____

SOCIAL STUDIES

Understand a Time Line

As you learned, a **time line** is a diagram. It shows you events in the order in which they happened. Time lines help you understand and remember the sequence, or time order, of events.

Quickly look through, or skim, the article for dates. Write the events on the lines below to complete the time line. The time line is started for you.

January 1839 — Sengbe Pieh kidnapped

June 1839 — _____

August 1839 — _____

September 1839 — _____

March 1841 — _____

November 1841 — Captives sail home

Telling Fact from Opinion 97

LESSON 8: Telling Fact from Opinion

Recognize Fact and Opinion

As you've read, a **primary source** is a record made by the people who lived during an event.

When the *Amistad* captives arrived in America, they spoke no English. They were unable to tell their side of the story or to understand why they were jailed. Four children were among the captives. While they awaited trial, they were taught to read and write. One of them, a young boy named Kale, quickly learned to speak and read English. He wrote the letter below to his lawyer, John Quincy Adams. Read the letter and answer the questions.

January 4, 1841

Dear Friend Mr. Adams:

I want to write a letter to you because you love Mende people, and you talk to the grand court. We want to tell you one thing. Jose Ruiz say we born in Havana, he tell lie. We all born in Mende. . . .

We want you to ask the Court what we have done wrong. What for Americans keep us in prison? Some people say Mende people crazy; Mende people dolt [a foolish person]; because we no talk American language. America people no talk Mende language; America people crazy dolts?

They tell bad things about Mende people, and we no understand. Some men say Mende people very happy because they laugh and have plenty of eat. Mr. Pendleton [the man who runs the jail] come, and Mende people all look sorry because they think about Mende land and friends we no see now. Mr. Pendleton say Mende people angry; white men afraid of us. The Mende people no look sorry again. That's why we laugh. But Mende people feel sorry: O, we can't tell how bad. Some people say Mende people no have souls. Why we feel bad we no have souls?

. . . We want you to tell court that Mende people no want to go back to Havana, we no want to be killed. Dear Friend, we want you to know how we feel, Mende people think, think, think. Nobody know what we think; the teacher he know, we tell him some. Mende people have got souls . . . All we want is make us free. . . .

A sketch of Kale.

List one **fact** from the letter.
_____
_____

List one **opinion** from the letter. Circle the clue word that identifies it as an opinion.
_____
_____

SOCIAL STUDIES

 **Compare Fact and Opinion**
Read the sentences below. Decide which sentences are facts and which are opinions. Write **F** for fact and **O** for opinion.

A sketch of Sengbe Pieh.

1. ____ The captives were kept in chains while in the ship's hold.

2. ____ The Africans were foolish to rebel against the "Amistad" crew.

3. ____ "Amistad" means "friendship" in Spanish.

4. ____ Jose Ruiz and Pedro Montes bought 52 slaves in Havana.

5. ____ Lieutenant Commander Gedney was frightened by the slaves.

6. ____ Sengbe Pieh thought he would never return to his homeland.

7. ____ The "Amistad" left Havana, Cuba, and headed for Puerto Principe.

8. ____ Sengbe led the rebellion.

9. ____ Abolitionists believed they could win in the courts.

10. ____ The young boy Kale learned to speak and write English.

Telling Fact from Opinion

LESSON 8
Telling Fact from Opinion

Charting the Facts

As you think about "Give Us Freedom," what information was most important to you? Use the chart below. Write which *facts* were important to you in the left column. Write why they were important in the right column.

Important Facts	Why Facts Were Important

Now write a brief letter to a friend explaining what you found important in the article. Use the information from the chart above.

Date

Dear _____,

_____

_____

_____

_____

_____

Your friend,

_____

Level E • Lesson 8

GETTING READY

Understanding Documents

Documents are anything written or printed that provide information or facts. Diaries, letters, maps, photographs, and artwork are examples of documents. To interpret these documents, you need to look carefully at all the details, think about what the symbols mean, and read all captions and titles.

LESSON 9

Think About Documents

Documents are either primary or secondary sources. A **primary source** is a record made by people who lived during an event. They took part in or saw this event. Old photographs, artwork, diaries, and journals written or printed at the time of the event are examples of primary sources. These sources record what happened during an event.

Secondary sources are documents created by people who were not present during the event. They created the material after the event happened. To interpret documents, ask yourself the **5Ws and H**:

- **Who** are the characters or people pictured in the document? **Who** was the original audience?
- **What** is it about? **What** is its purpose? **What** do I already know about the time period of the document?
- **Why** was the document created? **Where** and **when** was it created?
- **How** does the document relate, or connect, to its time?

Think About the Topic

Use the information in **Think About Documents** to decide if the following documents are primary or secondary sources. Write **primary** or **secondary** next to each sentence.

1. A diary written in 1775 about the American Revolution.

   _____

2. A painting created in 1980 showing the Spanish conquest of Mexico.

   _____

3. A story about Benjamin Franklin written by his great-grandson.

   _____

4. Photographs of immigrants taken in New York City tenements.

   _____

Understanding Documents 101

LESSON 9 Understanding Documents

STRATEGIES•TEST PREP
- Understand Documents
- Interpret Cartoons/Photographs
- Recognize Point of View
- Use Study Skills

Understanding Documents

Understand Political Cartoons/Posters

Political cartoons and posters are drawings that make people think about current events. They express the opinion of the artist. Artists sometimes use words in the artwork. They also use many symbols. A **symbol** is a design or an object that stands for something else. For example, a tall thin man with a beard named Uncle Sam is a symbol for the United States.

Artists create **political cartoons** to express an opinion or show a point of view. **Posters** are often used as advertisements or as propaganda, which is information that is spread to change the way people think or act. Artists give clues to help you understand the meaning of a cartoon or poster. Look for clues in the title and captions, in the symbols used, and in the details.

Follow these steps to help you understand political cartoons and posters:

- Study the poster or cartoon. Think about the subject. What event or issue is the cartoon or poster about? Study the characters. What are they doing?
- Read the caption. It tells you what the artwork is about. Identify objects or people in the cartoon. Look for important dates or clues that tell you when the artwork was done.
- Look for symbols. Are the people or objects symbols that stand for something else?

This poster was created during World War I. It was used to enlist people into the United States Army.

WRITE HERE

1. What does the symbol in the poster stand for? _____

2. What event inspired this poster? _____

3. What is the main idea of this poster? _____

Understand Political Cartoons

In 1845, Texas became the twenty-eighth state of the United States. Mexico did not accept the Rio Grande as the border between the two countries. Tension grew, and in 1846 Mexico attacked American forces along the Rio Grande. President James Polk declared war on Mexico. Thousands enlisted to protect the new state of Texas. Most of them were young Irish immigrants. Look at the cartoon. The volunteer soldiers stand at attention in the cartoon. The young officer standing in front of them wears a monocle, a type of eyeglass with only one lens. Wealthy men often wore monocles to look important. Think about what this detail tells you about the officers that were to lead the men into battle.

Volunteers join the army to fight the Mexican War.

Study the cartoon and answer the questions.

1. What is the issue or event shown in the cartoon?
   _____

2. List the characters in the cartoon and briefly describe them.
   _____
   _____

3. What is the artist saying about the officer and the soldiers? Are they ready for war?
   _____
   _____

Understanding Documents

LESSON 9: Understanding Documents

Interpret Political Cartoons

Look at the political cartoon titled "The American Rattlesnake" on page 105. In April 1782, this cartoon was published in London, England. It is about the American Revolution. The cartoon shows a rattlesnake wrapped around two units of British soldiers. The British generals Burgoyne and Cornwallis commanded these units. Cornwallis was trapped at Yorktown, Virginia, by George Washington's army. The French navy joined the American forces against the British. The French navy blocked the British navy from aiding Cornwallis. As a result, the British soldiers were unable to receive military support by land or sea. On October 19, 1781, Cornwallis surrendered to George Washington. The British surrender was a victory for the American colonists and ended the American Revolution.

The rattlesnake was an early symbol for the colonies. It was also used on flags before the stars and stripes. The words below the cartoon tell you that many people in England felt sympathy for the American cause. Study the cartoon. Fill in the chart below and answer the questions on the next page.

Subject: First look at the cartoon as a whole. Then identify the subject. Read the title and the message, or caption, under the cartoon. Briefly describe the subject.	
Symbols and Details: Look for important symbols and details. If there are any characters, what are they doing? How do they look? For example, who or what does the snake in this cartoon stand for?	
Message: Interpret the message. What has the snake done to the British forces? Why do you think the last circle has a sign that says, "Apartment to Let (rent)"?	

104 Level E • Lesson 9

SOCIAL STUDIES

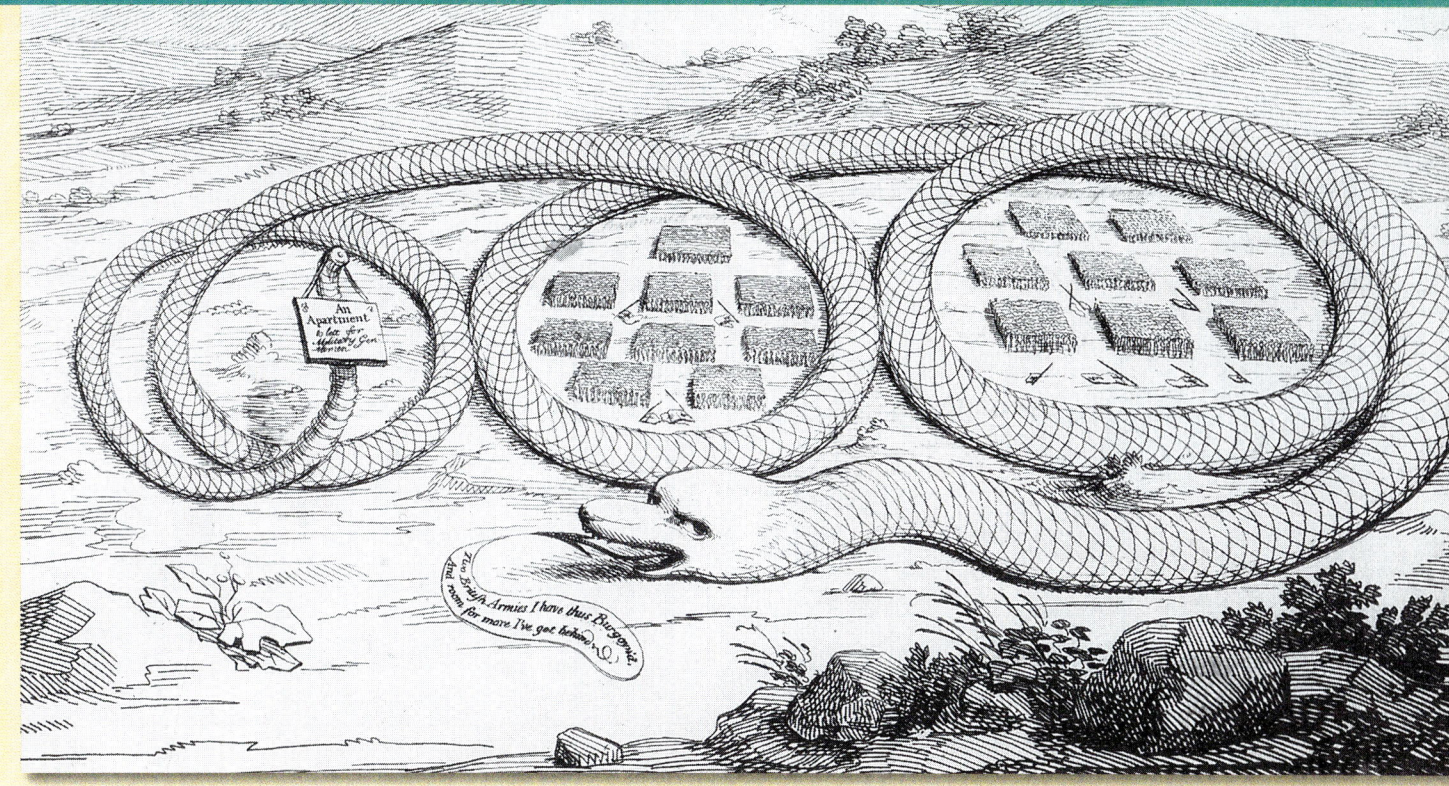

"The American Rattlesnake"

WRITE HERE

1. What is the event that this cartoon describes?

   _____

   _____

2. Why do you think the artist used the title "The American Rattlesnake" for this cartoon?

   _____

   _____

   _____

3. A British artist drew this cartoon. What is the artist's point of view, or opinion, about the event? Use details from the cartoon to support your answer.

   _____

   _____

   _____

Understanding Documents 105

Lesson 9: Understanding Documents

profits the money left after all the costs of running a business have been subtracted from all the money earned.

Interpret Political Cartoons

Railroads brought more and more settlers to the West. These settlers wanted land for farming and mining. To support the settlers, the United States government began to take land used by Native Americans. The government forced many Native American tribes to live on government land called reservations. The government hired officials, called agents, to manage the reservations. Some of these Indian agents were greedy and dishonest. They took government money, supplies, and land meant for Native Americans. As a result, most Native American families did not have enough food or clothing. They could not grow much food because the soil on the reservations was not good for farming.

Many Native American tribes were angry. They left the reservations and raided the settlers' land. General Nelson Miles was called in to put down the rebellion. During the 1870s and 1880s, Miles led successful battles against many Native American tribes, defeating leaders such as Geronimo, Sitting Bull, and Chief Joseph.

The political cartoon on the opposite page is titled "The Reason of the Indian Outbreak." In 1890, it appeared in the magazine *Judge.* In the cartoon, a thin, ragged Native American holds a musket, or rifle, and a package labeled "starvation rations." A **ration** is a "limited amount or share, especially of food." The Native American stands next to a well-dressed, fat Indian agent carrying bags of money.

Study the cartoon and fill in the chart below. Then answer the questions on the next page.

Portrait of Sitting Bull, taken about 1890.

Who are the characters or people in the cartoon?	What objects are used as symbols?

106 Level E • Lesson 9

SOCIAL STUDIES

"The Reason of the Indian Outbreak"

WRITE HERE

1. List three symbols you wrote in the chart on page 106. Explain what they mean.

   a. _____

   b. _____

   c. _____

2. What does the caption "starvation rations" mean on the package?

   _____

   _____

3. Write a brief description of the Indian agent in the cartoon.

   _____

   _____

4. Think about the meaning of this cartoon. What is the artist telling you about how the Native Americans were treated by some Indian agents? Use details from the cartoon to support your conclusion.

   _____

   _____

Understanding Documents 107

LESSON 9 Understanding Documents

🧩 Understand Photographs

Photographs are valuable records of people, places, and events from the past. Photos tell a story without words. Follow these steps to understand what the photographer is telling you about the subject.

- Carefully study the photograph. What is it saying about the topic? You can read a photograph just like a book, from left to right, and then up and down. Ask yourself what is happening in the picture.

- Divide the photograph into four sections. Look for new details in each section. Carefully look at the people, objects, and activities in the photograph. If there are people in the photograph, ask yourself what they are doing. Notice how they are dressed. Try to determine when the photograph was taken. You can often guess the date by the subject or by how people are dressed.

- Finally, ask yourself what story the photographer is telling you.

Carefully study the photograph on the opposite page of a general store in New Mexico. It was taken by a photographer named A. J. Buck, but the exact date of the photograph is not known. Think about the story the photograph tells. Complete the chart below and answer the questions on the next page.

People: Who are the people? How are they dressed?	Activities: What are the people doing? Why are they there?
_____	_____
_____	_____
_____	_____
_____	_____

SOCIAL STUDIES

People gather outside a general store in New Mexico.

WRITE HERE

1. This photograph was probably taken in the late 1800s or early 1900s. What details in the photograph help you know that this date is probably correct?

   _____

2. Look at the way the people are dressed. What does the clothing tell you about the people?

   _____

   _____

3. What is the name of the store?

   _____

4. What else does the store do besides sell goods?

   _____

5. List three items from the photograph that might be for sale in the store.

   _____

   _____

Understanding Documents

LESSON 9: Understanding Documents

Recognize Point of View in Photographs

Some photographs express a **point of view**, or opinion, about a problem. The photographer of this photo, taken in the early 1900s, wanted to call attention to a problem. He wanted to change public opinion.

When you look at a photograph, think about how it makes you feel and what story it tells you. The photograph below shows an immigrant family living in a New York tenement building. Study the photograph and complete the chart on the next page.

An immigrant family living in one room takes in laundry to make money.

People:	Activities:
Who are the people? How are they dressed?	What are the people doing? Why are they there?

Using the notes in your chart, answer the questions below.

WRITE HERE

1. Describe what you see in the photograph.

2. How are the people dressed?

3. Based on what you know about the lives of immigrants and the information in the photograph, why do you think that the photographer took this picture?

Understanding Documents 111

LESSON 9: Understanding Documents

Interpret Photographs

Photographs like this one describe events that happened in the past. In Chapter 1, "Laura Ingalls Wilder and the American Frontier," you learned about the Homestead Act. This law gave free land in the Great Plains to settlers. But these settlers faced many hardships: droughts, plagues, and starvation. From about 1900 into the 1930s, farmers in the Great Plains plowed the land over and over. When crops weren't growing, the land was bare. The drought dried the land out. Wind picked up the soil and blew it hundreds of miles away. The Great Plains became known as the Dust Bowl. The once rich land became dry and useless to farmers.

Study the photograph. Then answer the questions.

This photo from about 1937 shows an abandoned farm in the Dust Bowl.

WRITE HERE

1. What detail tells you that many farmers are having problems with their farms?
   _____
   _____

2. Do you think these farmers could sell their land? Why or why not?
   _____
   _____
   _____

NET CONNECTION
http://www.americaslibrary.gov and
http://www.nhptv.org/kn/vs/socla8h.htm

GETTING READY

Hernando Cortés

Hernando Cortés (kohr-TEZ) was a famous Spanish explorer. He is called the "conqueror of Mexico" because he defeated the Aztec empire. Cortés was a clever and ruthless leader. Both his enemies and his soldiers feared and admired him. But fate also played a role in his success. This is the story of his life and his actions in the New World.

Think About Taking Notes

Your goal for **taking notes** is to organize the information you read so that you can use it to help you study. To take notes, follow these steps:

- Skim the article to get a general idea of what it is about. Think about *what* you are reading *while* you are reading. Read with a purpose by keeping in mind the **5Ws and H**, *who, what, when, where, why,* and *how*. This is called **active reading**.

- Next, read the article carefully. Use note cards to write questions and answers as you read. If you can mark on the page, highlight important information or make a note in the margin. Keep your notes brief. Don't use complete sentences. Use short phrases. Use your own words. Use symbols and abbreviations: *w/* for "with"; *&* for "and"; *=* for "equals." You may also want to make a **graphic organizer** or an outline.

- Everyone has trouble with names and places they cannot pronounce. Don't try to pronounce the word each time you read it. If you do, you may forget what you are reading about. Instead, just pronounce part of the word. For example, the capital city of the Aztecs, Tenochtitlán, is hard to pronounce. Just say "Teno" as you read.

Think About the Topic

Reread the introduction to "Hernando Cortés" above. What do you think you will learn about in this article?

_____
_____
_____
_____
_____
_____
_____
_____

You have just written your first note. Taking notes is important because you can separate the more important parts of an article from the less important parts. Notes help you organize your ideas so that they make sense to you.

Taking Notes 113

Lesson 10: Taking Notes

STRATEGIES•TEST PREP
- Question
- Take Notes
- Understand Cause and Effect
- Identify Main Idea/Supporting Details
- Make an Outline
- Identify Sequence of Events
- Use Study Skills

Question
The first step in taking good notes is to ask good questions. Use the **5Ws and H** to help you. Begin by turning the headings into questions. As you read, write down the answers to your questions. Here is an example of what your notes should look like.

Hernando Cortés

A Young Dreamer

Young Hernando Cortés did not hear his teacher call on him in the classroom at the university in Spain. His mind was far away. He didn't want to study law. At fourteen years old, Hernando Cortés dreamed of glory and gold. Like his father, the young Cortés wanted to be a soldier.

Cortés was born in 1485. He grew up in the small town of Medellin, Spain. There were few opportunities for excitement or adventure. His father was a nobleman, but the family had little money. They struggled to send their son to school.

In the early 1500s, many schoolboys in Spain dreamed of traveling to a far-off land called the New World. The young Cortés believed that this new world would bring him riches and fame.

The New World

In 1504, at the age of nineteen, Cortés set out to fulfill his dream. He became a soldier and sailed from Spain to the New World. The ship landed on the island of Hispaniola. This island was the key location for Spain in the West Indies, not far from the coast of Cuba. The governor of the island liked the young soldier and gave him land and slaves. Cortés set up a farm and used the slaves to work his land.

Who was the Young Dreamer?
- Hernando Cortés
- studied law/didn't like
- wanted to be soldier
- born 1485, Medellin, Spain
- believed new world = riches/fame

Helpful Hint
Another way to take notes is to highlight the information. Notice that the above information is also highlighted in the article.

By 1511, Cortés was restless for new adventures. He decided to sail with Diego Velázquez (vuh-LAS-kuhs) and others to conquer Cuba for Spain. When Velázquez became governor of Cuba, he made Cortés the mayor of Santiago, a city in Cuba.

In his new position, Cortés gained more wealth, land, and slaves. He married a Spanish woman named Catalina Juarez. Cortés stayed in Cuba and forced his slaves to work even harder. Although he became wealthy, he was not satisfied. He wanted more and more wealth. He wrote in a letter, "I have come to win gold, not to plow the fields like a peasant."

A New Adventure Begins

In Cuba, the Spanish heard stories about a wealthy empire in Mexico. This empire had an **abundance** of gold and precious jewels. Cortés persuaded Velázquez to send him to Mexico with a fleet of ships. As Cortés left the dock, Velázquez shouted at him to stop the ship. Velázquez was worried that Cortés would take all the gold and glory for himself. But Cortés, pretending not to hear him, sailed away.

SOCIAL STUDIES

abundance (uh-BUN-dunss) plentiful; more than enough.

Take Notes

Now it's your turn to take notes from the information on this page. Write a *brief* note that answers each main idea question below. Don't use complete sentences, and use your own words. Notice that your answers are the details that support the main idea questions. Notes are highlighted in the article for the first question.

Heavy Spanish galleons built for war carried soldiers, cannons, and horses to Mexico.

WRITE HERE

1. What happened in Cuba?

2. What new adventure begins for Cortés?

LESSON 10

Taking Notes

An Unknown Land

In 1519, ten ships with about 500 Spanish soldiers, ten brass cannons, and 16 horses landed on the coast of Yucatan in Mexico. The native people were afraid and amazed at these strange white men with beards.

The natives had never before seen ships, cannons, or horses. The horses frightened the natives most of all. Before the Spanish introduced the horse, this animal was unknown in the New World.

At first, Cortés became friends with a Spanish priest who lived among the native people and spoke their language. The priest told Cortés about a great city surrounded by water that was filled with riches. This city was Tenochtitlán (tay-nahch-tee-TLAHN), the capital of the Aztec empire. The ruler's name was Montezuma (mahn-tuh-ZOO-muh).

At about this same time, Cortés met Doña Marina. She was the daughter of a powerful Indian chief. She was sold into slavery when her father died.

The Aztec capital city Tenochtitlán.

Understand Cause and Effect

Cause and effect answers the questions *What happened* and *Why did it happen*. The **cause** is the reason something happens. The **effect** is the result of what happens. To remember facts, use cause and effect. Look for reasons (causes) that explain why and what things happen (effects).

WRITE HERE

The author says that the native people had never seen horses before (cause). What *effect*, or result, did this have on the native people?

_____

_____

_____

116 Level E • Lesson 10

SOCIAL STUDIES

A drawing of Montezuma, in the Museum of Madrid, Spain.

Doña Marina was given to Cortés as a gift and quickly became a valuable member of his group. Without her help, Cortés may not have conquered the Aztecs. She spoke the Aztec language and knew their customs. Doña Marina learned Spanish and became Cortés's interpreter and teacher.

Cortés was determined to march inland and capture the Aztec capital with its treasure for Spain. Many of the soldiers were afraid to march into Tenochtitlán. They worried that the Aztec warriors outnumbered them. The soldiers had also heard stories that the Aztecs were fierce fighters.

Cortés realized that some of his soldiers wanted to return to Cuba. But he wanted so much to find this city of riches. Cortés burned all the ships, except for one. Now his solders had no choice. They could not return home. The soldiers had to stay and fight with him.

Take Notes Using Cause and Effect

Using cause and effect in your notes helps you understand and remember historical facts, details, and events. As you take notes, think about why things happen and what happens as a result.

WRITE HERE

List one *cause* that explains why the soldiers were afraid to march into the Aztec capital of Tenochtitlán.

_____
_____
_____

Taking Notes

Taking Notes

Cortés, dressed in a full suit of military armor, meets the ruler of the Aztecs, Montezuma. He welcomes Cortés wearing a splendid ceremonial robe, headdress, and shield made of bird feathers.

Take Notes Using Supporting Details

The **main idea** is the most important idea in a paragraph. **Supporting details** support, or build on, the main idea. Good notes include main ideas and details that support those main ideas.

Cortés the Conqueror

On August 16, 1519, Cortés began the 250-mile march into the Aztec capital. As he traveled across Mexico, his soldiers fought and won many battles. Their weapons and horses helped defeat thousands of Indian warriors. These warriors belonged to tribes who were the enemies of the Aztecs. Because Cortés was brave in battle, he earned the respect of these tribes, and they joined with him to fight against the Aztecs.

In early November of 1519, Cortés arrived at the Aztec capital. Montezuma and other Aztec leaders met him on a walkway into the city. "Welcome," they said, "we have been waiting for you. This is your home." The Aztecs believed that a fair-skinned god with a beard was supposed to return to them from the East. By chance, Cortés arrived in the same year that the Aztecs thought this god would return. The Aztecs believed that Cortés was this god.

WRITE HERE

The main idea of the paragraph is that the Aztecs welcomed Cortés and his men. Why? List two details in the paragraph that support, or explain, why the Aztecs acted this way.

1. _____   2. _____

Understand a Map

As a military leader, Cortés needed to share information with his soldiers and warriors from different Indian tribes. He drew a map. A map is a good way to organize and show information. No matter what language people speak, most understand a map.

This is a map of Tenochtitlán, the capital city of the Aztecs. The city was an island in the middle of a lake. Several paths called causeways connected the city to the shore. Cortés and Montezuma met on one of the causeways into the city.

lake   city square   causeway

1. Why do you think the author includes this map in the article?

_____
_____
_____

2. Explain how this map helped Cortés move his soldiers and the Indian warriors into Tenochtitlán to conquer the Aztecs.

_____
_____
_____

LESSON 10 Taking Notes

Take Notes Using the 5Ws and H

Be an active reader. As you read "The Conquest of Mexico," ask questions using the **5Ws and H**. Find the answers to the questions below as you read. You will use this information when you make an outline on the next page. Highlight the answers as you read or make a note in the writing area below. The first answer is marked for you.

- **W**ho is "The Conquest of Mexico" about?
- **W**hat events took place?
- **W**hen did the events take place?
- **W**here did the events take place?
- **W**hy did Cortés take Montezuma prisoner?
- **H**ow did Cortés capture Montezuma?

The Conquest of Mexico

In 1519, Cortés entered the capital for treasure and glory, not for kind words from the Aztecs. The Aztecs honored him with a beautiful palace in Tenochtitlán.

In a bold move, Cortés and his officers went to Montezuma's palace. They made Montezuma a prisoner. Cortés then demanded treasure. Montezuma gave Cortés bars of pure gold and a large amount of jewels. But this only increased his greed for more gold.

Montezuma greets Cortés.

While Cortés was in Tenochtitlán, Velázquez sent a new leader from Cuba to replace him. One of his soldiers warned Cortés that the man had landed in Mexico. Cortés left the capital to face his rival. They fought, and Cortés defeated him.

When Cortés returned to the Aztec capital, he discovered that Montezuma was dead. In 1520, a new Aztec leader attacked Cortés and his men and drove them from the city. But Cortés gathered an army of warriors who were enemies of the Aztecs. He marched on the city again. On August 13, 1521, Cortés finally conquered the great Aztec empire of Mexico.

WRITE HERE

Cortés and Aztecs

SOCIAL STUDIES

Take Notes Using an Outline

One of the best ways to organize ideas and information is to use an **outline**. It helps you understand the most important ideas in an article. It also helps you keep your notes brief. Outlines use numbers and letters to show main ideas and supporting details.

Outline the part of the article called "The Conquest of Mexico." Each paragraph becomes a capital letter. The first two paragraphs are outlined for you. Use facts from the article to complete the outline for the last two paragraphs.

I. The Conquest of Mexico

   A. Cortés

      1. 1519 entered Aztec capital

      2. looks for treasure/glory

      3. Aztecs gave him palace

   B. Montezuma

      1. made prisoner by Spanish

      2. gave Cortés gold/jewels

   C. Cortés leaves capital

      1.

      2.

   D.

      1.

      2.

      3.

Taking Notes

LESSON 10: Taking Notes

jealous to want something that someone else has; to be upset with someone because they seem more successful.

plea to appeal, argue, or defend a point of view.

Take Notes Using Sequence

When you need to remember dates, make a time line that shows the sequence of events. **Sequence**, or time order, is the order in which events happen. Always recite your notes aloud. You will remember much more of the information.

Read "After the Conquest." Highlight the dates. Then describe what happened on these dates. Keep your notes brief. The time line is started for you.

After the Conquest

Cortés spent the next several years rebuilding the city, which he renamed Mexico City. He sent gold and silver to Spain. Because of the riches Cortés won for Spain, the king made him governor and captain-general of Mexico.

Cortés was a hero to Spanish soldiers. He brought them glory and riches. But Governor Velázquez was **jealous** of Cortés's popularity with the military. As a result, he took Cortés's land and slaves in Cuba and Hispaniola while Cortés was in Mexico. Some of his friends were even put into prison.

Hernando Cortés, the conqueror of Mexico.

Cortés was angry about this treatment. In 1528, he returned to Spain to ask for the king's help. But the king was also jealous of Cortés. The king listened to Cortés's **plea** and gave him new titles and honors. But the king took away his political power.

The next year Cortés returned to Mexico and continued his explorations. He traveled north and discovered the peninsula of California. But he missed having real power. In 1541, he returned to Spain for the last time. Because Cortés used much of his own money to pay for his explorations, he was in debt. When Cortés asked the Spanish government to repay the money, the king and his court ignored him. His pride was hurt, and he went to live alone in a small village near Seville, Spain. The great Spanish conqueror of Mexico died a poor man on December 2, 1547.

NET CONNECTION
http://www.cybersleuth-kids.com
(type *Hernan Cortes* in the search box)

WRITE HERE

1528	Cortés returns to Spain/asks King's help w/ land
1529	_____
1541	_____
1547	_____

122 Level E • Lesson 10

SOCIAL STUDIES

Understand Main Idea and Supporting Details

The **main idea** is the most important idea in a paragraph. Other sentences in the paragraph **support**, or help explain, the main idea. Understanding main ideas and supporting details helps you find important information and take better notes.

Below is a list of sentences that make up a paragraph. The first two sentences and the last two sentences are numbered for you. Number the other sentences that support the main idea in the correct order. Remember that these sentences explain or expand the main idea. To make an organized paragraph, these sentences should follow the main idea in an order that makes sense.

After the Conquest

____1____ After Spain's victory over Mexico, what happened to the Native Americans?

_____ These diseases were unknown to the Native Americans, who had no defense against them.

_____ But the Spanish also had another ally in their war—disease. Most Native Americans died from diseases brought to the New World by the Europeans.

____2____ In less than fifty years of Spanish control, the Aztecs, Incas, and many smaller tribes were destroyed.

_____ Many Aztecs and Incas died in battles fought against the Spanish.

_____ The Spanish carried the germs of smallpox, yellow fever, and typhoid.

____7____ When Cortés first arrived in 1519, more than 25 million Native Americans lived in Mexico.

____8____ Less than 100 years later, wars and disease had killed almost 24 million natives, or about 95% of the population.

Taking Notes **123**

Taking Notes

Take Notes About "Hernando Cortés"

Use this page to take notes about the biography "Hernando Cortés." First, look back at all the headings in the article. Turn each heading into a question. Leave space between each question for your notes that answer the questions. Think about the 5Ws and H when you answer each question. Remember, your notes should be brief! Use abbreviations in your notes. List only the most important information. The first question is started for you.

Montezuma and Cortés meet in Tenochtitlán. The artist believed that the Aztec capital looked like a European city.

Who was the Young Dreamer?

- Cortés, born 1485, Spain
- studied law/didn't like
- wanted to be soldier
- believed new world = riches/fame

Part 1 Multiple-Choice Test

Directions for Questions 1-16:

This part of the test has 16 multiple-choice questions. Each question is followed by four answer choices, labeled A through D. Read each question carefully. Decide which choice is the correct answer. Use a pencil to fill in the circle that has the same letter as the answer you have chosen.

Read the **sample question** below:

> **Sample Question**
>
> Each star on the American flag stands for a
> - Ⓐ state.
> - Ⓑ colony.
> - Ⓒ senator.
> - Ⓓ country.

The correct answer is **state**, which is next to the letter **A**. Fill in the circle that has the letter **A**.

Answer all 16 questions on Part 1 of this test. Fill in only one circle for each question. Be sure to erase completely any answer you want to change. You may not know the answers to some of the questions, but do the best you can to answer each one.

**When you have finished Part 1, go on to Part 2.
Now begin Part 1 of the test.**

1. The Homestead Act gave citizens, who lived on the land for 5 years, 160 acres of free land in the Great Plains. You can conclude that the Homestead Act
   - Ⓐ failed to attract people to the Great Plains.
   - Ⓑ decreased the population of the Great Plains.
   - Ⓒ increased the population of the Great Plains.
   - Ⓓ increased the population of northeastern states.

2. Which is an example of a primary source about the American Revolution?
   - Ⓐ an article in your history book about the United States
   - Ⓑ a biography about George Washington
   - Ⓒ a painting done in 2000 of a battle during the American Revolution
   - Ⓓ a journal written by a soldier who fought in the American Revolution

3. When people share the same language, customs, and beliefs, they usually have the same
   - Ⓐ appearance.
   - Ⓑ culture.
   - Ⓒ democracy.
   - Ⓓ union.

4. The process by which water turns into water vapor is called
   - Ⓐ condensation.
   - Ⓑ precipitation.
   - Ⓒ evaporation.
   - Ⓓ absorption.

Base your answers for 5 and 6 on the map below.

5. Which imaginary line divides the earth into the Northern and Southern Hemispheres?

   Ⓐ the North Pole

   Ⓑ equator

   Ⓒ prime meridian

   Ⓓ the hemispheres

6. What continent is located entirely in the Northern and Eastern Hemispheres?

   Ⓐ Australia

   Ⓑ North America

   Ⓒ Asia

   Ⓓ Antarctica

7. The main purpose of a political map is to show
   - Ⓐ countries and borders.
   - Ⓑ mountains and rivers.
   - Ⓒ climate and natural resources.
   - Ⓓ population growth.

8. The main function of the United States House of Representatives and the Senate of the federal government is to
   - Ⓐ decide if a law is constitutional.
   - Ⓑ enforce laws.
   - Ⓒ elect the president.
   - Ⓓ make laws.

9. The early colonists saw land as a means to wealth and power. The Native Americans saw land as something
   - Ⓐ to be owned and developed.
   - Ⓑ that can be mined.
   - Ⓒ to be bought and sold.
   - Ⓓ that provides food and life.

10. Cool grasslands, temperate forests, and high mountains can best be described as
    - Ⓐ temperatures.
    - Ⓑ plants.
    - Ⓒ biomes.
    - Ⓓ deserts.

Base your answers for 11 and 12 on the circle graphs below.

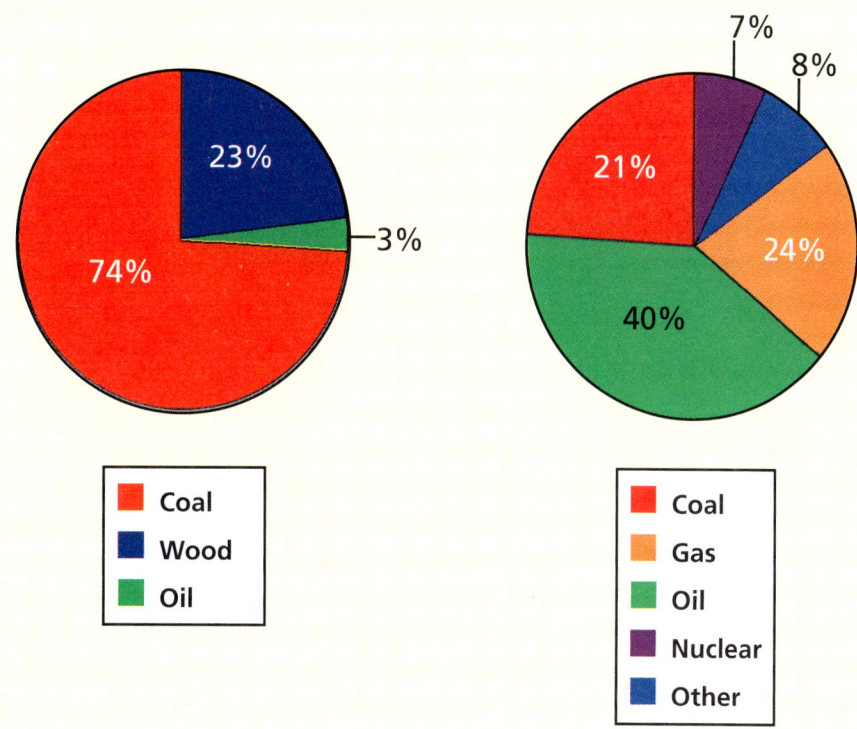

11. In 1900, what kind of energy did most people use?
    - (A) coal
    - (B) gas
    - (C) oil
    - (D) wood

12. When you compare the two graphs, which statement is the best conclusion?
    - (A) In 1900, people did not like to use oil.
    - (B) In 1998, most people relied on nuclear energy to provide electricity.
    - (C) The use of oil in the United States has increased by 37% since 1900.
    - (D) The use of coal has decreased by 30% since 1900.

13. Because many immigrants arriving at Ellis Island were too poor to move to other parts of the country, they
    - (A) returned to their homelands.
    - (B) moved into New York City.
    - (C) stayed at Ellis Island.
    - (D) were sent to the midwestern states.

14. Most early settlements developed next to oceans or rivers because
    - (A) farmland was nearby.
    - (B) the railroad ran close to the towns along the coast.
    - (C) colonists could use ships to import and export goods.
    - (D) colonists did not want to travel too far inland.

15. Which statement is an opinion?
    - (A) U.S. citizens like the two-party system.
    - (B) The U.S. federal government has three branches.
    - (C) U.S. citizens vote for a president every four years.
    - (D) Citizens of the U.S. pay taxes.

Base your answer to question 16 on the partial outline below.

```
I. _____
   A  Chile
   B  Argentina
   C  Brazil
   D  Peru
```

16. Which heading belongs after Roman numeral I?
    - (A) Provinces in Canada
    - (B) Countries in South America
    - (C) Native American Tribes in North America
    - (D) Religions in Asia

Assessment

 **Part 2 Constructed-Response Test**

Directions

Write your answers to the questions that follow on the lines provided in this book.

Base your answers for the questions on the picture. The picture is called "The Oregon Trail." You learned about the Homestead Act and life on the American frontier in Lesson 1 of this book.

1. What is the subject of this picture? [1]

   _____

2. Write **two** reasons why these pioneers traveled together in such large groups. [2]

   a. _____

   b. _____

3. Write **two** reasons why pioneers wanted to travel to the frontier. [2]

   a. _____

   _____

   b. _____

   _____

Base your answers to questions 4 through 6 on the map of the Oregon Trail below and what you learned about maps in Lesson 3.

Pioneers in the 1840s traveled west by covered wagon along the Oregon Trail. Families, like Laura Ingalls Wilder and her family, followed the trail to claim free land. The 2,000-mile Oregon Trail began in Independence, Missouri, and ended near Astoria, Oregon.

"Line of Original Emigration to the Pacific Northwest Commonly Known as the Old Oregon Trail" from *The Ox Team or the Old Oregon Trail 1852-1906* by Ezra Meeker. Fourth Edition 1907.

4. Study the map of the Oregon Trail. List two natural barriers that the pioneers faced as they traveled along the Oregon Trail. [2]

   a. _____

   b. _____

5. Find Wyoming on the map. What mountain range did the pioneers cross to reach Idaho? [1]

_____

6. Explain **two** problems other than natural barriers that the settlers may have faced traveling on the Oregon Trail. [2]

   a. _____

   _____

   _____

   _____

   b. _____

   _____

   _____

   _____

Base your answers to questions 7 through 10 on the bar graph below. The graph shows the states with the largest populations of Native Americans. You learned about graphs in Lesson 5 of this book.

Use the bar graph to answer the questions.

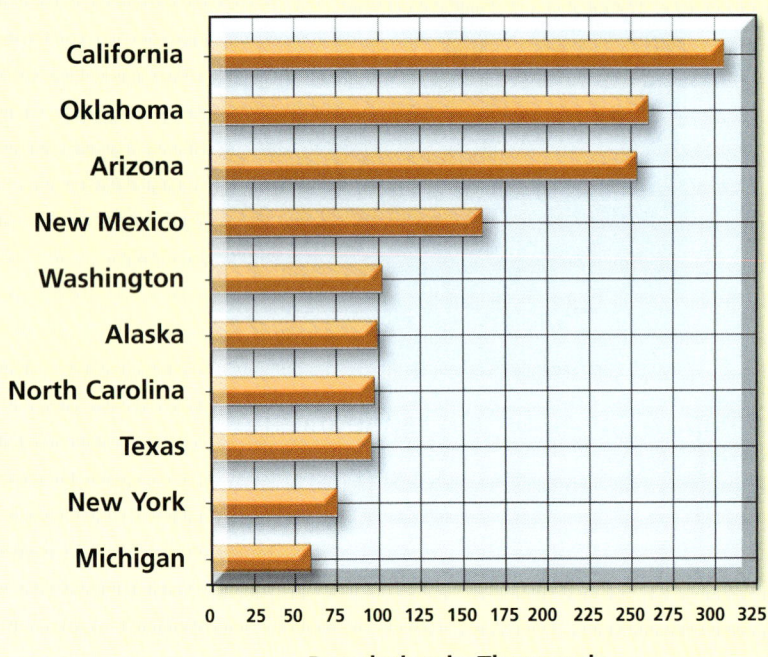

States with Largest Populations of Native Americans, 1999

Population in Thousands

Source: Census Bureau Facts for Features American Indian Heritage Month 1999.

7. When was this information for the bar graph collected? [1] _____

8. List **two** states that have a Native American population under 100,000. [2]

   a. _____

   b. _____

9. In what region of the United States do most Native Americans live? [1]

   _____

10. Look at the graph and title. How can you tell that the states listed are not the only states with Native American populations? Explain your answer. [2]

    _____

    _____

 Part 3 Document-Based Question Test

Directions

The task below is based on documents 1 through 4. This task tests how you work with historical documents.

Historical Background

In the 1600s, thousands of British immigrated to America looking for a better way of life. These new settlers found plentiful natural resources.

Task

Part A: Short-Answer Response. This part of the test contains four documents. Study each document carefully. Then answer the question or questions following the document. These answers will help you write your essay.

Part B: Essay. Use the information from the documents, your answers to the questions in Part A, and your knowledge of social studies and science to plan and write a well-organized essay.

- In your essay, explain how the natural resources in America were important to the survival of the settlers and to the development of the colonies.

Part A Short-Answer Questions

Directions: Study each document carefully. Answer the question or questions that follow each document in the space provided.

Document 1

1. State **two** natural resources in this photograph. [2]

   a. _____

   b. _____

2. State how one of these resources could be used by the colonists. [1]

   _____

Document 2

When European settlers arrived in America, they found a land rich in natural resources. There were vast forests with a variety of trees, such as pine, oak, and maple. Colonists used handsaws and axes to cut the trees. Horses and oxen then dragged the trees from the woods to a river. The logs floated down the river to sawmills. At the sawmill, water was used to generate power to cut the logs into boards. Colonists used wood to build carts and barges for hauling products. Settlers also used wood for heating, cooking, and building. In many colonies, such as Boston, New York, and Charleston, South Carolina, shipbuilding became an important industry. Colonists used trees to build ships. English merchants bought ships to carry products back and forth between the colonies and England.

3. Explain **two** ways the forests were an important natural resource used by the colonists. [2]

   a. _____

   b. _____

Document 3

4. Choose **three** objects and explain how each one was used in daily life to help the colonists survive in the New World. [3]

Object	How It Was Used in Daily Life
1.	1.
2.	2.
3.	3.

Part 3 Document-Based Question Test 137

Document 4

5. Based on this drawing, explain **two** ways in which ships were important to the colonists in America. [2]

   a. _____

   _____

   _____

   b. _____

   _____

   _____

Part B

Essay

Directions: Write a well-organized essay using the information in the documents, the answers to the questions in Part A, and what you know about colonial America. Use the space below to organize your notes.

Notes

_____
_____
_____
_____
_____
_____
_____
_____
_____

Task: Explain how the natural resources in America were important to the survival of the settlers and to the development of the colonies. Using the lines below and on the next page, write your essay.

_____
_____
_____
_____

GLOSSARY

Boldfaced words within the definitions are other terms that appear in the glossary.

American Revolutionary War   a war fought for the independence of the American colonies from Great Britain, 1775-1783.

axis   a line of information at the side of a graph (vertical axis) or at the bottom of a graph (horizontal axis).

bill   a document presenting a new law. Bills are debated in the United States **Congress,** state legislatures, and at the local level.

biome   a region of the world that is defined by its **climate** and the unique plants and animals that are there.

caption   a short title or description printed below a graphic, or visual, display of information.

Chinese Exclusion Act   a law passed in 1882 that banned Chinese immigration for ten years.

climate   the yearly pattern of average temperatures, rainfall, winds, and hours of sunlight in an area.

condensation   the process by which a gas changes into a liquid.

continent   one of the seven large landmasses of the earth. The seven continents are Asia, Africa, Europe, North America, South America, Australia, and Antarctica.

colony   a territory (land) governed by a foreign nation.

community   a group of people who live in the same area or who share the same interests.

GLOSSARY

Congress the government body of the United States that makes laws. It is made up of the **Senate** and the **House of Representatives.**

culture the common way of life, ideas, customs, and traditions shared by a group of people. Their culture may include a common language.

democracy a way of governing a country in which the people choose their leaders in elections.

equator an imaginary line around the middle of the earth that is halfway between the North and South poles. The equator divides the earth into the Northern and Southern **Hemispheres.**

evaporation the process by which a liquid changes into a gas.

executive branch the branch of government that carries out and enforces the laws.

hemisphere one half of the globe. See **equator** and **prime meridian.**

Homestead Act passed in 1862. This law offered 160 acres of free land to anyone who agreed to live on and improve the land for five years.

House of Representatives part of the **legislative branch** of the federal government. It is the lower house of the United States **Congress.** The House members are popularly elected representatives. The House is responsible for making policies and laws.

immigrant a person who settles in a new country.

judicial branch the branch of government that interprets laws. The judicial branch is made up of the **Supreme Court** and other federal courts.

landforms the different shapes that make up the earth's surface, such as mountains, plains, canyons, and plateaus.

latitude imaginary lines that run east and west on a map or globe. These lines give the position of a place on the earth, measured in degrees north or south of the **equator.**

legislative branch the branch of government that makes up the nation's laws. The legislative branch is made up of the **Congress** (the **House of Representatives** and the **Senate**).

longitude imaginary lines that run north and south on a map. These lines give the position of a place on the earth, measured in degrees east or west of a line that runs through the Greenwich Observatory in England. Lines of longitude are drawn on a map or globe from the North Pole to the South Pole.

map key place on a map that shows the meaning of the map symbols. Also called a map legend.

natural resource a material found in nature that is useful to people. Lumber, minerals, and water are some natural resources.

Pilgrim a member of the religious group that rejected the Church of England. The Pilgrims sailed to America and established Plymouth Colony, in present-day Massachusetts, in 1620.

precipitation water that falls from the sky in the form of rain, sleet, hail, or snow.

primary source materials or information written or made by people who lived during the time that an event occurred.

GLOSSARY

prime meridian an imaginary line around the earth. It runs north and south through Greenwich, England. The prime meridian divides the earth into the Eastern and Western **Hemispheres.**

Proclamation of 1773 a law in which the British prohibited the American colonists from settling west of the Appalachian Mountains.

R

recycle to reuse old or used items, such as glass, paper, plastic, and aluminum cans, so that they can be used to make new products.

S

secondary source materials or information about an earlier time or event written or made by people who lived in a later time.

Senate part of the **legislative branch** of the federal government. It is the upper house of the United States **Congress.** Two senators are elected from each state. The Senate is responsible for making policies and laws.

state political and geographical units that make up a country. The United States has 50 states.

Supreme Court the highest and most powerful court in the United States. The Supreme Court is made up of nine justices who have the power to overturn decisions made in lower courts and can declare laws unconstitutional. A state Supreme Court is the highest court in that state.

U

United States Constitution the written document containing the political principles by which the United States is governed.